Dave Doroghy | Graeme Menzies

111 Places
in Whistler
That You Must
Not Miss

emons:

This book is dedicated to the memory of the great Canadian author Jake MacDonald. He entered my life at just the right time and left much too early. Thanks for your encouragement, advice, and friendship.
Dave Doroghy

To my former headmaster Col. Amyas Biss, who once observed that those insufficiently gifted with academic prowess might yet succeed if sufficiently endowed with character.
Graeme Menzies

© Emons Verlag GmbH
All rights reserved
Photographs by Dave Doroghy and Graeme Menzies, except see page 238
Cover icon: shutterstock.com/Svetlana Foote
Edited by Karen E. Seiger
Layout: Editorial Design & Artdirection, Conny Laue,
based on a design by Lübbeke | Naumann | Thoben
Maps: altancicek.design, www.altancicek.de
Basic cartographical information from Openstreetmap,
OpenStreetMap-Mitwirkende, ODbL
Printing and binding: Grafisches Centrum Cuno, Calbe
Printed in Germany 2021
ISBN 978-3-7408-1046-7
First edition

Did you enjoy this guidebook? Would you like to see more?
Join us in uncovering new places around the world on:
www.111places.com

Foreword

This isn't our first *111 Places* book, but it is the first one we've written during a pandemic. Like everyone else, we had to get extra-creative, we had to be persistent, and we had to be patient. We also had to be safe. At the beginning of the project, we thought the biggest threat to our health would be bears – not a virus! On our first book, we reviewed each other's ideas face-to-face. On this project, many of our meetings were done screen-to-screen or conducted behind masks … like a couple of book-writing gangsters.

With the writing and photography all done, our hope now is that readers will soon be able to get out and explore the places we've put in this book. Take a hike, have a meal, sample a brew, be amused, be challenged, and be entertained. We've found plenty for you to see and do in and around Whistler, the four-season wonderland.

When we wrote *111 Places in Vancouver That You Must Not Miss*, we felt it needed this Whistler version to accompany it. The two towns and their surrounding regions complement each other so well. Fortunately, our publisher agreed with us. We now feel like the picture is complete. From Vancouver to Whistler, with stops in between and beyond, these are the places that comprise our portrait of Whistler with 111 fun, quirky, beautiful, stunning, historic, hidden, tasty, and tantalizing marvels of Canada's West Coast.

For Dave, who has been visiting Whistler since he was a teenager and has a condo at Whistler's base, this has been an opportunity to share some of his favorite tales and tips – especially those relating to winter and skiing. For Graeme, a frequent visitor to Whistler since he and Dave both worked together on the 2010 Winter Olympics, writing this guidebook provided the perfect opportunity to explore further afield and discover summertime *off-piste* pursuits.

We hope you enjoy this book with friends in good health.

111 Places

1— 1968 Olympic Bid Display

You win some, you lose some

Olympic fans know that the 1968 Winter Games took place in Grenoble, France. A much lesser known fact is that Whistler took a run at hosting those Games. An excellent outdoor display case in Creekside tells the story of this first bid in great detail. In fact, Whistler has bid for the Olympics domestically and internationally several times. The International Olympic Committee's (IOC) decision on June 2, 2003 finally brought home the grand prize: the 2010 Winter Games. Part of the reason that the 2010 bid was successful was because much of the infrastructure to stage one of the world's biggest sporting events already existed here.

The exact opposite can be said for that first bid that began picking up steam in 1960. After the Winter Olympics that year in Squaw Valley, California, a group of Vancouver-based businessmen began dreaming and scheming about staging the games eight years later on what was known then as London Mountain (today's Whistler). They named their booster group GODA, an acronym for the Garibaldi Olympic Development Association. They worked like the storied "little train that could," plugging away for years as they pursued their vision with an "I think I can, I think I can, I think I can" attitude.

Getting Whistler ready for the 1968 Games would have been a Herculean task. The main way to reach the small settlement back then was, of course, by train. All of the venues and facilities had to be built from scratch – not just the sporting venues, but the hotels, athletes' village, a water supply system, sewers, sewage disposal, a substation for power supply, a fire station, and a hospital. GODA's bid was not successful, but they would not quit. In 1968 they submitted another bid to host the 1972 Olympics. They lost to Sapporo, Japan; they bid once more for the 1980 Games, and lost again. And then in 2003, under a different name, they landed the 2010 Games.

Address 2063 Lake Placid Road, Whistler, BC V0N 1B2 | **Getting there** From the Sea to Sky Highway, exit at Lake Placid Road. The plaque is near the Starbucks. | **Hours** Unrestricted | **Tip** Across the street from Creekside Village is a small plaza with a restaurant that has the best poke bowls this side of Hawaii. It's a cheap and cheerful little place called Whistler Samurai Bowl (2011 Innsbruck Drive, www.seatoskysamurai.com).

2_3 Singing Birds
Small wonders

The most unusual thing you'll find at 3 Singing Birds is the shop itself. This isn't the sort of shop where you always know what they have on the shelves. It's more like a curated gallery of things that, while constantly changing, are also always focused on unique, ethically produced, small-batch, sustainable products.

Globe-trotting owner Paula Jeffers, who moved to Whistler from the Bahamas, opened this neighbourhood store a few years after the 2010 Olympics and still takes frequent trips abroad to research and discover new items. She visits trade shows in places like New York, Los Angeles, and Paris, and she imports products made by local artisans in faraway places like India, Italy, and beyond. So when you enter 3 Singing Birds, you'll find an usual assortment of goods, from hand-dyed local yarns to diamond rings to Blackwing pencils. Or you might find locally made, organic Hollow Tree Candles – each one scented to celebrate British Columbia's timbered bounty. These candles have incredible scents and creative names like "Canoe" (pine needles, birch-bark resin, and juniper wood), "Lumberjack" (santal, fir needle, and cedar resin), and of course "Hollow Tree" (western red cedar).

The number of brands represented in the store numbers in the dozens – from A Punto B's timeless and simplistic clothing to Yuketen's handmade footwear and luggage. Inventory changes throughout the seasons, so no return trip to the store is exactly the same as the one before. And that's part of what makes this a place not to miss, whether you're a local or a visitor.

Speaking of visitors, the shop not only has unique items on the shelves, it sometimes has unique personalities walk through the door. British style icons Victoria and David Beckham ("Posh & Becks") have paid a visit, as have US actors Owen Wilson and Woody Harrelson, and Canadian music star Sarah McLachlan.

Address 112–4340 Lorimer Road, Whistler, BC V8E 1A5, +1 (604) 862-3726, www.3singingbirds.com, info@3singingbirds.com | **Getting there** From the Sea to Sky Highway, exit onto Lorimer Road. Turn right just past the intersection and park at Marketplace Shopping Centre. The shop is at the south end of the parking lot. | **Hours** Daily 10am–6pm | **Tip** Satisfy your sweet tooth with a detour to The Great Glass Elevator Candy Shop a few paces away (115–4350 Lorimer Road, www.whistlercandyshop.com).

3 A-Frame Brewing
Craft beer, off the beaten path

Is the quintessential Canadian A-frame cottage a place or is it an attitude? Can the cottage lifestyle be sustained year-round instead of just for a few weeks each summer? If it had a flavor, could you put it in a bottle? These are the questions Jeff Oldenborger and Caylin Glazier decided to test when they opened A-Frame Brewing in 2016, and they are still working on those questions today. Because this husband and wife brewing team knows life's too short to spend dreaming about the cottage life, they want to live it every day. That's what this hyper-local brewery is all about, and that's why you shouldn't miss it.

So do yourself a favour: slow down, relax, and take the time to discover this off-the-beaten-path destination that locals in the know and outdoor adventurers cling to like the Grand Wall of the Stawamus Chief (see ch. 24). Visiting this brewhouse, complete with its outdoor fire pit, log stools and tables, is almost like visiting your cool neighbours at the lake. They have a locally handmade, wooden "Okanagan Lake playtable" for your kids, they allow dogs (outside), and you can bring your own food too, though they have some great BC-made snacks you'll probably want to enjoy.

To help you really tap into the essence of the cottage, they've even named all their core beers after BC lakes, including the Okanagan Lake Cream Ale and the Magic Lake Porter. When you visit the cabin decor-inspired tap room, you can sample these brews and more by the glass or in flights. If you're on the go, pick up some cans, fill up your growler, or go big with a couple of 650ml 'Bomber' bottles of your favourite brew.

Jeff and Caylin don't just go about extolling the cottage ideal – they really do live it. Your chances of finding A-Frame beers in the big city are about as good as finding a moose walking down Granville Street, so make sure you visit when you're in the area.

NOT BEER

SORRY
GROWLERS
TEMPORARILY
UNAVAILABLE

ALL PRICES INCLUDE TAX

Address 1-38927 Queens Way, Squamish, BC V8B 0K9, +1 (604) 892-0777, www.aframebrewing.com, info@aframebrewing.com | Getting there From the Sea to Sky Highway, take the Industrial Way exit, then turn left onto Queens Way. | Hours Mon–Thu noon–10pm, Fri & Sat noon–11pm, Sun noon–9pm | Tip Chase that beverage down with authentic Mexican fare from the 1958 stainless steel Airstream food truck operated by Luz Tacos next to A-Frame's generous outdoor patio (www.luztacos.com).

4 Amos & Andes

When you need a new sweater

Amos & Andes, one of the smallest retail shops you've ever been in, is the perfect place to get your new sweater. At 188 square feet, this shop is officially the smallest retail shop in Whistler. Not only that, it is also Whistler's longest owner-operated business in the same location. So it's a small space but a big deal – a local landmark that you must not miss. Especially if you need a good sweater.

Shop owner Hilary Davison opened Amos & Andes in 1984 and comes by her sweater knowledge growing up on a farm in the UK, where the best way to beat the winter chill was to put on another sweater.

Over the years, thousands of sweaters have made their way from the shelves of Amos & Andes to the shoulders of Whistler residents and visitors alike. During the 2010 Winter Olympic Games, one of the hottest items in the shop was the official Winter Olympics sweater made by Dale of Norway. Dale had been outfitting the Norwegian Olympic ski team since 1956 and created the red sweater made famous by Canadian ski legend Nancy Greene at the Grenoble Games in 1968 (see ch. 1). In celebration of the 100th anniversary of Canadian alpine skiing, that iconic red gem was re-released by Dale in 2019, and you too can get one at this shop. It was no surprise that members of the Norwegian royal family visited the shop during the 2010 games.

In addition to the traditional Norwegian sweaters, Amos & Andes has traditional sweaters from other sweater-loving places too: Sweden, Ireland, Cowichan Valley, Serbia, and more. And in addition to Norwegian royals, Hollywood royals have visited the shop over the years, including Jennifer Aniston, Shannon Tweed, and Susan Sarandon.

When the snow starts to fall and the weather gets chilly, everyone knows there's no better way to warm up than with a new sweater made with natural fibres, purchased in the heartland of Canadian Winter Olympic history.

Address 4321 Village Gate Boulevard, Suite 2, Whistler, BC V8E 1H3, +1 (604) 932-7202, www.whistlersweatershop.com, hilary@whistlersweatershop.com | **Getting there** From the Sea to Sky Highway, exit onto Village Gate Boulevard. Turn right and park. Walk past the Whistler Visitor Centre, onto Village Stroll, and turn left. | **Hours** Daily 11am–6pm | **Tip** Florence Petersen Park is just a five-minute walk north of here, and a cosy outdoorsy place to wear your new sweater (4325 Main Street).

5_ "Arfa" Lake Dog Park
At Lake Alpha

Dogs like running around off leash, jumping off docks into a lake, and playing with other dogs. Dogs like hanging with their owners. That's why dogs like Whistler and its amazing, totally chill dog culture. Sometimes it feels like everyone living here has a dog – and that every visitor brings one too. It's easy to take your dog to Whistler. A quick search online revealed 15 dog-friendly hotels. And we're not talking about just the small inns – the list includes the Nita Lake Lodge, the Fairmont Chateau Whistler, and the Westin Resort. Many of these hotels have resident dogs that we'd like to say greet you as you arrive, but most of them just sleep on the floor by the hotel's check-in counters.

There are four off-leash dog parks at Whistler, and the large, enclosed, fenced area at Alpha Lake is one of the best. It has the added feature of a super cool, 30-foot-long dog dock, where excited dogs can get up enough speed to launch themselves into the air for 10 feet and land in the water. Pure dog joy. There is a sand pit for digging too. It's a local favourite because the official civic wayfinding signage that helps you locate it along the Valley Trail lists it as "Lake Arfa." Get it? Arf Arf Arf.

Then there's the dog-friendly dining aspect of Whistler. It gets a bit trickier here though. Technically, provincial health laws prohibit bringing dogs into any restaurant in BC. But many restaurants in Whistler have outdoor patio seating, and some of them have gotten around the health laws by allowing patrons to sit on their patios' perimeters, with their dogs leashed and resting on the other side.

Finally, what do you do with Fido when you go skiing? That's where Whistler draws the line. Pooches are not allowed to run below you up the chairlift line or to follow you down the mountain as you ski. So look for one of the several doggy daycare centers in town.

Address Lake Placid Road, Whistler, BC V0N, www.whistler.com/activities/lakes-beaches-parks | **Getting there** From the Sea to Sky Highway, exit at Lake Placid Road going east. | **Hours** Daily 5am–9:30pm | **Tip** After some unrestricted romping in Arfa Park, why not throw a leash on your dog and head north on the Valley Trail to the Nita Lake Lodge nearby. They have a great little coffee shop there where you can sit outside with Rover (2131 Lake Placid Road, www.nitalakelodge.com).

6 __ Armchair Books
The best bookstore in Whistler

You might think Armchair Books is named for the comfy armchair you sit in while you read a favourite book, but you'd be wrong. Whistler's only bookstore is actually named after the Armchair Glacier that towers above the resort and sort of looks like the back of an armchair. The clever name was the idea of bookstore founder Hazel Ellis, who opened the bookstore in 1979. Back then it was a small affair – just 300 square feet of retail space. And Whistler, which only became officially incorporated as a Resort Municipality in 1975, was much smaller too. As the municipality thrived and grew, so did the bookstore.

In the mid-1990s the store doubled in size, and today it stocks bookshelves across 111 square metres (1,200 square feet) of space. All that growth has happened without moving from the original location. So when you visit Armchair Books, you're also visiting one of the oldest businesses in its original location. You'll also be visiting a real second-generation family business, as Hazel's son Dan Ellis took over daily operation of the bookstore in 1998. And on busy days, you might also see the rest of their family pitching in to provide that old-time customer service you thought was just lost to history.

Armchair Books has something for everyone to read. Many customers stop by to pick up a good holiday read – a spy novel, a biography, the latest new release, and chart-toppers – while adventure-seekers come in for the trail maps, ski guides, and outdoor lifestyle books. Whistler is a foodie town, so this is also a great place to select a new cookbook. And the kids' section is always popular with local and visiting families.

The real treasure is not what's on the shelf, though. It's the help and advice you get shopping in an intimate store where the owner has hand-picked everything and can help you find what you're looking for even if you're not sure what that is.

Address 4205 Village Square, Whistler, BC V0N 1B4, +1 (604) 932-5557, www.whistlerbooks.com, armchair@whistlerbooks.com | **Getting there** From the Sea to Sky Highway, exit onto Village Gate Boulevard and take your first right onto Gateway Drive, then right again onto Whistler Way. Park at the Rainbow public parkade. Village Square is a short walk away. | **Hours** Daily 9am–7pm | **Tip** The COWS ice cream shop is a short walk away. Try a scoop of the caramel moocchiato or cownadian bacon (4313 Main Street, Unit 1, www.cows.ca).

7 __ Art Junction
The art of living

A lot of people who live in the mountains march to the beat of their own drum. In Harvey Lim's case, he also works and plays to the beat of his own drum. Literally. When you enter his Function Junction gallery, your eyes will be drawn to the red drum kit that sits almost centre stage, surrounded by a vibrant and diverse collection of works by nearly 50 artists from up and down the Sea to Sky corridor and around British Columbia.

Art Junction is a kaleidoscopic feast for the eyes. Gaze past the drum kit, and you'll see a colourful selection of works representing a variety of styles and subjects – from Vicki English's stunning acrylic scenes featuring the West Coast's natural wonders, to Alli Van Gruen's portraits of chairs, to Kris Robinson's dog portraits, to Patrick Leach's hand-crafted, museum-quality pottery depicting landscapes, pictographs and basket-weaving designs inspired by his Coast Salish community heritage. To browse this eclectic gallery is to browse the creative output of those who both live in and love the awe and wonder of the world around them.

Like many of the artists whose works are displayed at Art Junction, Lim's life started elsewhere before ending up here. In Lim's case, the journey began in England, where he was a professional soccer goalie for a number of teams, including Norwich City FC, Friska Viljor FC in Sweden, and Sing Tao SC in Hong Kong, before eventually falling under Whistler's spell. Risking everything for the opportunity to live among the majesty of the mountains, he took a chance. That self-confidence – perhaps the kind only a soccer goalie truly knows – plus some good fortune, lead to ownership of Art Junction in 2004. Lim is also a skilled framer and can frame just about anything from an Olympic torch to a pair of antique cowboy chaps. So if there's something you've always wanted to get framed, this is the place to get it done.

Address 1068 Millar Creek Road, Whistler, BC VE8 0S8, +1 (604) 938-9000, www.artjunction.ca, info@artjunction.ca | Getting there Exit the Sea to Sky Highway at Alta Lake Road (Function Junction), cross the tracks, and turn left on Millar Creek Road. It's on your left. | Hours Tue, Thu, & Sat 11am−5pm | Tip Just a few steps away is Camp Lifestyle and Coffee. Great coffee, cool things to buy (1066 Millar Creek Road, www.camplifestyle.ca).

8   Athlete's Village
A low-cost housing solution

Visiting the modern Cheakamus Crossing community, where about 800 Whistler residents live, is a pleasant, hassle-free experience. In February of 2010, it was anything but that. Simply getting into the housing complex was like going through airport security, with numerous guarded checkpoints, bomb-sniffing dogs, little gray plastic trays to unload personal items onto, and more metal detectors than you could shake a magnetic wand at. The community was built to house 3,500 Olympic and Paralympic athletes and officials safely. At the time, it was packed with the world's greatest winter sport athletes caught between wanting to party and celebrate at any hour of the day or night while at the same time getting enough rest and nutritious food to perform at their peak levels. Suffice it to say, the place was teeming with nervous energy, international comradery, and a healthy dose of youthful enthusiasm.

The athletes loved the upscale, earth-tone apartment buildings, and the Resort Municipality of Whistler loved them too. After the games were over, the Municipality ultimately converted the Village into some much-needed, low-cost, permanent housing. Historically, past Olympic Games Organizing Committees have built temporary, removable accommodations or utilized hotel rooms or places like local university dorms to house their athletes. But the Whistler Council members came up with a better solution that addressed the chronic housing shortage that has plagued their city. The $145-million Athletes' Village, with its 221 affordable ownership units, 55 affordable rental units, 188 youth hostel beds, and 20 market-priced townhomes, was transformed into today's Cheakamus Crossing. This community is a lasting legacy of the 2010 Olympic Winter Games.

When you visit, be sure to drop by and see the spectacular $32-million Athletes' Centre, nestled in the middle of the neighborhood.

Address 1080 Legacy Way, Whistler, BC V8E 0K3, +1 (604) 964-0059, info@whistlerolympicpark.com | **Getting there** From the Sea to Sky Highway, exit onto Cheakamus Lake Road to Legacy Way. | **Hours** Unrestricted from the outside | **Tip** Between the Whistler Athlete's Centre and the Athlete Centre Lodge right next door are three excellent aboriginal art sculptures: a contemporary stainless steel, glass, and paint work by Carey Newman; a six-sided cube by Rosalie Dipcsu; and an Olympic Truce wall created by Corrine Hunt, Leo Obstbaum, and James Lee.

9 Audain Art Museum

Oh so audacious!

Usually, all the best art is gathered from various places and concentrated in city galleries and museums – the Louvre, the Metropolitan Museum of Art, or the National Gallery. But there's one gallery that took art away from the city and put it in the mountains. It's Whistler's Audain Art Museum.

Here you will find one of the world's finest collections of Northwest Coast First Nations masks and some of the best and most desirable British Columbian art, plus exhibitions from across Canada and the world. The museum is named after Vancouver home builder and philanthropist Michael Audain, who, with his wife Yoshiko Karasawa, built this 17,000-square-metre (56,000-square-foot) museum. It is the only museum in Canada with a permanent collection that exclusively represents the artists of its home province.

The story behind the museum is almost as stunning as the collection itself. Back in the 1960s, Michael Audain started his career as an intellectual, pursuing a Diploma from the University of Lyon in France, three degrees from the University of British Columbia (UBC), and post-graduate studies at the London School of Economics. As one might expect of 1960s intellectuals, he had a colourful life as a social activist. At UBC he founded the Nuclear Disarmament Club and organized its peace marches. He was a delegate at the 1961 founding convention of Canada's New Democratic Party and, that same year, travelled to the southern US states to become a Freedom Rider and was sentenced to a jail term and a $250 fine.

Over time, the intellectual, social activist, socialist, ex-con became an expert on housing policy and played a critical role in creating the Housing Corporation of British Columbia. By 1988, he was president of Polygon Homes and an established art connoisseur and philanthropist. Audain has honorary PhDs from five BC universities.

Address 4350 Blackcomb Way, Whistler, BC V8E 1N3, +1 (604) 962-0413, www.audainartmuseum.com, info@audainartmuseum.com | Getting there From the Sea to Sky Highway, take Village Gate exit and turn left on Blackcomb Way, then park at first right. | Hours Thu–Sun 11am–6pm | Tip Across the street from the Audain's front door is *A Timeless Circle*, created by Susan Point. The bronze sculpture represents the community's experience of hosting people from all over the world for the 2010 Winter Olympics (www.susanpoint.com).

10_ Be a Biathlete
Give it a shot

Have you ever imagined how easy or hard it would be to hit one of those little round targets you see biathlon athletes shoot during the Winter Olympics? For a small fee, you can find out at the Whistler Olympic Park. Instructors will guide you through the process and help you learn how to shoot a real biathlon rifle. You'll gain appreciation for a sport that few will ever try.

The word "biathlon" means "two contests" (much as the word "triathlon" means three contests, and "pentathlon" means five contests). In this case, the two contests are skiing and shooting. The origins of the sport are difficult to pinpoint – long enough ago that there were no sports marketing executives sitting around a table trying to invent a new sport with big merchandising and sponsorship appeal. Some say the sport goes back as far as 4,000 years. But the credit for the biathlon's modern format generally goes to the Norwegian military, which started an annual skiing and shooting event in 1912. The International Olympic Committee had a "military patrol" demonstration event at the 1924 Winter Olympics in Chamonix. At the 1948 Olympics in St. Moritz, the two events were part of an event called Winter Pentathlon, combining cross-country skiing with downhill skiing, shooting, fencing, and horse riding. But not all at once, of course – although that would be very entertaining.

The Whistler facility is a legacy of the 2010 Winter Olympics and is used by a wide variety of winter sport enthusiasts, including hardcore athletes training for future Olympics, and outdoor adventure groups like the Army Cadets, the Sea to Sky Nordics Club, and others. If skiing isn't necessarily your thing, you can still visit the facility in the summer (watch out for bears!) as well as in the winter. Regardless of the weather, if you just want to try and hit that little round target, this is the place to give it a shot.

Address 5 Callaghan Road, Whistler, BC V0N 1B8, +1 604 964-0059, www.whistlersportlegacies.com/whistler-olympic-park/things-to-do/biathlon | Getting there From the Sea to Sky Highway, exit Callaghan Road going north, drive 12 kilometres (7.5 miles) to Whistler Olympic Park. | Hours See website for seasonal hours | Tip Visit the Whistler Olympic Park Rental Shop to get fully kitted out in whatever you need for a day of cross-country skiing and snowshoeing that you'll remember for a lifetime (5 Callaghan Road, whistlersportlegacies.com).

11   Bear Spotting
Ask the bear if you can play through

About 100 bears live in Whistler. And since they are strong, unpredictable, and wild creatures with minds of their own, it's impossible to pinpoint exactly where to spot them on any given day. There are, however, some good places where your odds will increase.

But you must be very careful. Most bears at Whistler tend to mind their own business. But if you startle one or get between a mamma bear and her cubs, look out! Bears may bluff their way out of human encounters by charging and then turning away at the last second. Your calm behaviour reassures them that you are not posing a threat. Screams or sudden movements can trigger bear attacks. And never feed the bears. It's illegal and carries a stiff fine and possible jail time.

If, after all these warnings, you are still interested in bear spotting, check out one of Whistler's three golf courses. They are The Whistler Golf Course (4001 Whistler Way), the Nicklaus North Golf Course (8080 Nicklaus North Boulevard), and the Fairmont Chateau Whistler Golf Course (4612 Blackcomb Way). Whistler bears seem to like to hang out on these courses where they can interrupt play. It's a good thing though because they are easier to spot on the fairways than in heavily forested areas.

The courses have limited public trails beside them from which you can bear-spot, or you could of course just go and play a round of golf with some friends. Mountain bike trails make for good bear spotting too, and Whistler's Olympic Park (see ch. 10) is a place they seem to frequent often. You can also book a professionally guided, safe bear-spotting tour led by guides who have a strong understanding of local bear hang outs. Again, never run when you spot a bear! Now with all this said, it might be easier for you to just take a selfie next to the six-foot tall wooden "Bear Warning" sign there. It's easy to locate it at the Olympic Park.

If you meet me …

Do not gather around me (or my cubs).

Stay calm, don't run.

Back away slowly, give me space.

Never feed me.

Keep dogs on a leash.

#KeepOurBearsAlive

Learn more at
BearSmart.com

Proudly sponsored by

Address **Various** | Getting there **Various** | Hours **Various** | Tip Not far from that handy bear information sign is Escape Route, an aptly named store that sells something you may consider buying if you do go bear spotting: bear spray (113–4350 Lorimer Road, www.escaperoute.ca).

12 The Beer Farm

Golden brews, fresh from the farm

Way back in 1895, a teenage lad named W. M. Miller left Scotland for a series of adventures that would eventually conclude with him buying acres of lush, fertile land here in the Pemberton Valley. No one knows with absolute certainty, but family folklore says he got his start with the aid of a gold nugget found while prospecting in the Yukon. In any case, years of youthful wandering and adventure seeking took root here, and he started life anew as a potato farmer. Fast forward to 120 years later, and you'll find Miller's descendants still running that same farm and still growing potatoes using the same fresh, mountain-fed water source of the Birkenhead River. But now they also grow their own barley and hops and brew it on site into a unique offering of lagers and ales. It's the Beer Farm!

The fresh, natural ingredients produce a "locally grown beer" that carries a suitably hearty Heartland punch and a deep, rich flavor. You'll find none of that sissy, urban lite beer around here. The Canadian Golden Strong is a 7.5% brew strong enough to take the stripes off a lumberjack's shirt. Even the most delicate brew, the 4.2% Farmer's Daughter White, has enough kick to score a field goal. And, speaking of fields, the scenery is fantastic.

After you park on the grass near the old tractor and get your beer from the barn, you can sit outside and look at acres and acres of pastoral perfection. If polished beer marketing schemes dreamt up by Madison Avenue executives and urban hipsters have left you thirsting for the real deal, then come spend some time at the Brew Farm. No one brews beer like fourth generation farmers.

Although open year round, the Beer Farm is a perfect summer destination – a great place to relax and sit in the sun with friends old and new. The Beer Farm is family- and dog-friendly (dogs and kids drink free here – but only fresh water).

Address 8324 Meadows Road, Pemberton, BC V0N 2L0, +1 (778) 770 1523, www.thebeerfarmers.com | Getting there Birch Street, turn right on Prospect Street/ Pemberton Meadows Road, for 5 kilometres (3.2 miles). Look for the big sign on your right. | Hours See website for seasonal hours | Tip Visit or spend the night at the Pemberton Valley Inn, a cedar log home located on seven acres of beautiful farmland (1427 Collins Road, www.pembertonvalleyinn.com).

13 Big Bus, Big Dreams
Have a double espresso from a double decker

This story is the mountain version of the movie *Field of Dreams*. Only it's not a baseball diamond in a corn field, but rather Double Decker Coffee Roaster in the Callaghan Valley. Either way, owner Patrick Sills must have been hearing the winter winds whisper the epic line, "If you build it, they will come," when building this outsized monument to big buses and big dreams. And it was no small task. He purchased the bus in 2018, drove it from Victoria to Whistler, and then started months of grueling renovations – a colourful interior paint scheme, thick wood table tops, several cosy booths. He toiled through summer heat and winter cold right through to April of 2019.

Along the way, he studied the fine art of coffee roasting and took a road trip to Idaho to pick up the heavy Diedrich IR 2.5 kilo coffee roaster that is the powerhouse behind this mountainside micro coffee roastery and espresso bar. And while doing all this he was doing two other jobs – grooming snow in the winter and putting out wildfires in the summer. This is a coffee place you must not miss.

This particular bus began life in Liverpool in 1967, three years before that city's most famous foursome released a song about "the long and winding road that leads to your door." Perhaps its route even passed Strawberry Fields or went down Penny Lane. In any case, to borrow a lyric from Gerry and the Pacemakers, it eventually ferried across the Mersey and made its way to Victoria, where it served as a city transit bus before beginning a second career with a local sight-seeing company. The bus was retired and sitting with a mechanic in Sooke when Patrick came a-courting. He successfully coaxed the bus back onto the road to a ferry over the Salish Sea, to the Sea to Sky Highway, and to its new home here in the mountains of the Callaghan Valley. Day trippers will want to buy a return ticket to this place – and a hot cuppa for the road.

Address 1000 Callaghan Valley Road, Whistler, BC V0N 1B1, www.doubledeckercoffeeroasting.ca | **Getting there** From the Sea to Sky Highway, exit at Callaghan Road and drive 6.25 kilometres (3.9 miles). Pass the Alexander Falls lookout, then exit left at the "Ski Callaghan" sign. Go over the wooden bridge and look for the big red double-decker bus. | **Hours** Fri–Mon 9am–4pm | **Tip** Since you just passed it to get here, why not also visit Alexander Falls? There's a great scenic lookout just five minutes away (www.alltrails.com/trail/canada/british-columbia/alexander-falls).

14 The Birding Platform
Birds big and small at Alta Lake

When you pack your bags to head to Whistler don't forget to throw in a pair of binoculars. Birding might not be on the top of your list of things to do there, but you may want to consider moving it up a few notches, given the wide variety of species the lakes, forests, and subalpine regions attract. As you will soon learn, at Whistler they come in all sizes, shapes, and colours too.

Over 500 species of birds can be spotted in British Columbia, and the Whistler region accounts for about 260 of them. A good place to start adding new birds to your list is from atop the raised wooden birding platform at Alta Lake. Your odds of spotting something interesting there increases dramatically from the raised vantage point, a solid 3-metre (10-foot) structure on the north end of the lake, positioned in the perfect spot.

One species that is very distinctive and easy to recognize even without those binoculars is the trumpeter swan. A massive flock of them visits Whistler along their migration path every winter. They are very big, snow-white, and hard to miss. Alta Lake is also known as "Swan Lake" because it attracts so many of them. This magnificent, elegant creature is the largest North American wildfowl and the second heaviest flying animal on the planet. They weigh about 9 – 14 kg (21 to 30 lbs) each. You may have to look a bit harder to spot, at the other end of the spectrum, the acrobatic adventures of one of the several varieties of hummingbirds that live in the area. They are amongst the smallest birds in the world, with an adult hummingbird tipping the scales at about the same weight as a single almond.

The viewing platform at Alta Lake gives you an unobstructed view which is good because hummingbirds are the only species of bird in the world that can fly both backwards and sideways. Unlike the swans, hummingbirds never stay in one place for very long.

Address The birding platform is located at the north end of Alta Lake, 5 kilometres (3 miles) north of Rainbow Park, www.whistler.com/activities/lakes-beaches-parks | **Getting there** From the Sea to Sky Highway, exit at Alta Lake Road and drive approximately 5 kilometres (3 miles) to Rainbow Park. | **Hours** Unrestricted | **Tip** Enjoy an early morning bird walk with Whistler Naturalists. They start at the bottom of Lorimer Road at Valley Trail the first Saturday of every month (www.whistlernaturalists.ca).

15 The Brackendale Eagles
World Eagle Capital

Where is the best place in Canada to view bald eagles? That's easy: Brackendale. This unassuming little village on the way up to Whistler holds the record for the largest number of bald eagles spotted in one day, allowing it to lay claim to the title, "World Eagle Capital." Who would have imagined that the iconic, time-honored American symbol of freedom and glory prefers to hang out north of the border.

Every year, an annual bald eagle count is held in Brackendale on the first Sunday in January, where up to 40 experienced birders volunteer to spot, document, and celebrate sightings of *Haliaeetus leucocephalus,* the great bird's scientific name. One day in 1994, a record-breaking 3,769 of the magnificent creatures were counted. Just to manage expectations, that year was a bit of an anomaly, as since then, the average number of recorded sightings of this large raptor on the first Sunday of the year is approximately 1,300.

Keeping track of all the eagles – and not double counting them – is a challenge. The birders spend a day visiting a total of 20 locations in the area, using rafts, skis, and snow-shoes to get around. Then, at the end of the day, near a blazing, wood-burning fireplace inside the Brackendale art gallery, a tally is posted on an old school chalkboard as the results are released to the public.

The eagles are of course attracted to the smorgasbord of salmon spawning in the Squamish River – to be more specific, chum salmon. They catch these fish on the river's sand bars and roost in the cottonwood trees along the shores. Although you can spot eagles in Brackendale and the surrounding area year-round, the best time to see them is between mid-November and mid-January, and the best time of day to see them is from sunrise till around 10:00am. In the afternoon, they are likely to be soaring high above and are harder to spot. Don't forget your binoculars, and wear something warm.

Address 41015 Government Road, Brackendale, BC V0N 1H0, +1 (604) 815-4994, www.exploresquamish.com/explore/brackendale-eagles-provincial-park, info@tourismsquamish.com | **Getting there** From the Sea to Sky Highway, take the Depot Road exit, then turn left on Government Road, and follow the signs. | **Hours** Unrestricted | **Tip** The Brackendale Art Gallery is definitely worth a visit after you have spotted an eagle (41950 Government Road, www.brackendale art gallery.com).

16 Bob Barker's Fight Scene
The Happy Hole at Furry Creek

One of the most memorable scenes from *Happy Gilmore,* one of Adam Sandler's most loved movies, took place here on the ninth hole of the Furry Creek Golf and Country Club. The movie features Adam Sandler as Happy Gilmore – a hockey player who uses an outrageous slapshot-style golf swing to earn prize money on the golf circuit to pay off his grandmothers' back-taxes and save her from losing her home to the auction block.

Furry Creek's 6,000+ yards of playable twists and turns through rainforest and ravines make it one of the most scenic golf courses in British Columbia, if not in all of Canada. Other films have shot at this location, including *Romeo Must Die*, and the TV series *Backstrom*. The ninth hole is called "Happy's Hole."

In the Furry Creek scene, Sandler's character is paired with *The Price is Right* game show host Bob Barker, playing himself, in a fictional Pro-Am match. The two argue over Gilmore's bungling of the match, and soon their sassy backtalk devolves into a full blown brawl, with 73-year-old Barker dominating the 30-year-old Sandler with a flurry of body blows and several left hooks. The scene is so memorable, the YouTube clip has over two million views. But Barker's moves should be no surprise – he has a black belt in Karate and studied Tang Soo Do karate under the direction of Chuck Norris! Apparently he did his own stunts in this scene. Maybe that's one reason why it won the first-ever MTV Movie Award for "Best Fight."

The view of Howe Sound from Sandler's career-boosting Happy Hole is gobsmacking. Take a moment to notice the Japanese design influences on the club's art and architecture, nods to the course's original visionaries. See and experience the club's Sea to Sky Restaurant, plan an event at their Waterfall Terrace, or visit the well-stocked Golf Shop for some unique mementos of this very happy place.

Address 150 Country Club Road, Furry Creek, BC V8B 1A3, +1 (604) 896-2224, www.furrycreekgolf.com, info@furrycreekgolf.com | Getting there From the Sea to Sky Highway, exit on Furry Creek Drive and follow the signs. | Hours Daily 9am–3pm | Tip For the full Sea to Sky golf experience, round out Furry Creek's sea views with the stunning sky views found at Pemberton's Big Sky Golf Club (1690 Airport Road, www.bigskygolf.ca).

17 Britannia Shipwrecks

Explore the mysteries of this watery graveyard

The waters off Britannia Beach contain a large variety of marine life, including lingcod, large schools of striped perch, dungeness and decorator crabs, plumose anemones, sea cucumbers, sea stars, prawns, tube worms, barnacles, and kelp. And this shoreline is also a ship graveyard.

The decommissioned Canadian Coast Guard vessel *Ready* rests directly across the road from the Galileo Coffee Company and 30 metres (100 feet) below the surface. She was a 29-metre-long (95-foot-long), twin-screw, diesel-powered search and rescue cutter, built in North Vancouver at Burrard Dry Dock in 1963. She had four sister ships: *Racer*, *Rally*, *Rapid*, and *Relay*. After she was decommissioned, CCG *Ready* was acquired by the Maritime Heritage Society of Vancouver in hopes that they could restore the vessel and make her a part of a floating maritime museum at Britannia Beach. But on January 17, 2011, she sank under mysterious circumstances.

Resting near the CCG *Ready* is another mystery: an unnamed ship. All that is known about this one is that it has all the masts, rigging, and holds used for fishing. She is wood-hulled with a steel wheelhouse, and she was probably built in the 1950s. The *Cape Swain*, believed to have sunk in the late 1980s, is wood-hulled with steel sheathing and also appears to be a seine fishing boat. It was probably built in the 1940s or 1950s and may have started life as something other than a fishing boat, undergoing a conversion later in life.

In deeper waters, wreck divers will find the wood-hulled *La Lumière*. Built in 1944 at Wheeler Ship Building Corporation and originally named USS *ATR-64*, she served as a US Navy rescue tug during World War II. After the war, she was decommissioned from the Navy and sold for commercial service. The 50-metre-long (165-foot) tug sank under mysterious circumstances on May 9, 2008. Today, it too rests on a slope not far from shore.

Address Howe Sound, Britannia Beach, BC V0N 1J0, www.britanniabeach.com/diving-in-britannia-beach, hello@britanniabeach.com | Getting there From the Sea to Sky Highway, take the Copper Drive exit at Britannia Beach. Take the pedestrian crosswalk over the highway and walk back south or to the shoreline to see the shipwrecks' final resting places. | Hours Unrestricted | Tip One of the abandoned docks you see nearby was featured as Captain Hook's Dock in the TV series *Once Upon A Time* (season 2, episode 4).

18 Britannia Mine Museum

A mine-blowing experience

Few things are cooler than an abandoned mine shaft. Literally. Wear a sweatshirt or several layers when you visit because once you get into one of these old mine tunnels, you'll be going someplace where the sun literally don't shine. Brrr!

The story of the mining operation and the community of Britannia is one of heroism and tragedy, perseverance and failure, imagination and tedium, and wealth and decline, and it's all revealed to you through a number of mind-blowing sensations at the Britannia Mine Museum.

The mine itself is named after the town of Britannia Beach, which itself is named after the mountain that dominates the town, which was named after a 100-ton frigate under the command of Capt. Richards, who was surveying the Colony of British Columbia's coast in 1859 for the British Admiralty. The rich mineral resources here were discovered shortly afterwards in 1888 by Dr. A. A. Forbes, and soon this would be the largest copper mine in the British Empire and home to some 60,000 people. Over the course of its lifetime, Britannia's mines would eventually surrender an impressive 1.2 billion pounds of copper ore, a quarter billion pounds of zinc, five million ounces of silver, 450,000 ounces of gold, and over 700,000 tons of pyrite to the industry, labour, and enterprise of the people who used to work and live here. They carved and blasted some 210 kilometres (130 miles) of tunnels into the foreboding rock. But the mine also took its toll. In its 70 years of operation, 98 people lost their lives underground.

Britannia's Mill 3, the Concentrator, was designated a National Historic Site in 1988 and is the main attraction on tours hosted by the Museum. The mines and vistas are so unique and cool they often show up in television shows and Hollywood movies, such as *Scooby-Doo 2: Monsters Unleashed*, the original *X-Files*, and *The Interview*, directed by BC's native son Seth Rogen.

Address 1 Forbes Way, Britannia Beach, BC V0N 1J0, +1 (800) 896-4044, www.britanniaminemuseum.ca | Getting there Take the Sea to Sky Highway to Copper Drive. Museum will be on your right. | Hours Daily 9am–4:30pm | Tip The Chatterbox Café, right next door to the mine's Admissions Office, is a nostalgic reproduction of the original café that served the local community back in the day, and a great pit stop before you get back on the road (1 Forbes Way, www.exploresquamish.com/business/chatterbox-cafe).

19__ Canada's Most Scenic Road

Curves meet chrome

For those motorists who believe life is about the journey, not just about getting to the destination, the Sea to Sky Highway offers one of the most beautiful, paved journeys in North America.

Several times a year, various car clubs take advantage of its many curves and astounding views. Even if you don't have a classic car yourself, keeping an eye open for these events can turn your personal road trip into a parade of wonders. The winding, bucolic highway is a magnet to motorists all year long. Organized events begin in the spring. Every May long weekend the All-British Whistler Run coaxes over a hundred British classics out of sleepy winter storage to create a cavalcade of chrome bumpers, curvy fenders, and throaty exhausts all the way up to its concluding awards ceremony at Whistler Creekside Plaza (see ch. 28). Look for classic cars from over 60 marques, including MG, Morgan, Triumph, Aston Martin, Jaguar, Bentley, and Rolls-Royce.

If Lambos, Maseratis, and Ferraris are more your speed, the luxury vehicles and supercars that take to the highway in June will catch your eye. The Hublot Diamond Rally bills itself as "Canada's largest collection and outdoor gathering of luxury and supercars on Canada's most scenic road." The event includes a private pitstop at Pemberton Airport, where participants in this charity rally lay rubber on the airstrip. In late August the BC Corvette Club takes to the Sea to Sky for their annual Wheels to Rails Run from Vancouver to Squamish. In September there's the Sea to Sky All-British Rally, and in October watch out for the Squamish-based Classic Car Adventures' annual Sea to Sky Thanksgiving Run, a meetup of pre-1979 classic cars and trucks, retro cars from the 1980s and 1990s, and other "vehicles of distinction." If you like curves, classics, and chrome, this is the highway to your heart.

Address The Sea to Sky Highway, BC, www.whistler.com/getting-here/road/conditions |
Getting there The highway runs between Horseshoe Bay in the south to Pemberton in
the north. | Hours Unrestricted | Tip A safe and stunning place to take an epic sea-to-sky
photo of your road trip is at the Porteau Cove Road Lookout. Take the Porteau Road exit
about 2 kilometres (1.25 miles) south of Porteau.

20 Cenotaph of Remembrance

Lest we forget

Every year, the Resort Municipality of Whistler, like every other community in Canada, stops everything on November 11 to remember those who came before us and made the ultimate sacrifice.

Old traditions run deep. Since the early 1980s, an impromptu ceremony took place every year at the Whistler Fire Rescue Service parking lot. Locals would gather there to lay wreaths at the site that was to be the future town cenotaph. There was no monument there until 1985, when the Whistler Rotary Club commissioned a small cenotaph to be erected at the Fire Hall. A stone from a quarry off of the Duffy Lake Road was laid near the hall to serve as a focal point for the communities' annual event and to honor those who served our country. The Fire Hall was the logical location for the cenotaph, since the annual November 11th event had grown there organically from the start. It was a local, centralized location that suited everyone, and it felt very appropriate in small-town Whistler.

As Whistler evolved and grew, so did its Remembrance Day Celebration; and as the years went by, more and more people attended Whistler's important annual observance in the parking lot. The event grew to include a parade, the service of remembrance, a helicopter fly by, and coffee and hot chocolate at the Fire Hall courtesy of the Rotary Club. The parking lot began to overflow, and finally the event outgrew its location and had to be moved, which sparked a bit of a heated debate. On November 11, 2017, a couple of firefighters at the Whistler Fire Hall were asked to stay behind. Rather than attend the ceremony, they redirected errant foot traffic to the new, less-crowded cenotaph location. Today look for the low-profile stone with brass plaques on both sides at Olympic Park.

Address Olympic Plaza, 4365 Blackcomb Way, Whistler, BC V0N 1B4 | Getting there From the Sea to Sky Highway, exit onto Lorimer Road and park off of Blackcomb Way. Cenotaph is on the outer ring of the Olympic Plaza. | Hours Unrestricted | Tip The 2010 Paralympic Games were staged at Whistler from March 12 to 21, 2010, and a wonderful sculpture of The Paralympic Games' equivalent to the Olympic rings is close by. Called the *Paralympic Agitos*, it's a large silver installation that you can't miss (www.whistler.ca/tour/137).

IN MEMORY OF
OUR HONOURED DEAD

WORLD WAR I	1914 – 1918
WORLD WAR II	1939 – 1945
KOREA	1950 – 1953
AFGHANISTAN	2001 – 2014

LEST WE FORGET – NOUS NOUS SOUVIENDRONS

21__The Cheakamus Community Gardens

Mountain air meets green thumbs

There's something about digging with your hands in the dirt that's good for the soul. And there's something about a great acronym that makes you appreciate the organization behind it – like the Association of Whistler Area Residents for the Environment (AWARE). One of AWARE's main ongoing initiatives is a welcoming community garden with over 100 1.2-by-2.4-metre (4-by-8-foot), wooden growing boxes. A little piece of gardening paradise in the shadow of Whistler Mountain will set you back $75 per year. And once it's yours, you can plant and grow anything you want. Well, make that almost anything you want – there are a few things that gardeners are asked not to plant: fruits, berries, corn, or anything else that will attract bears or wildlife. And no invasive species.

The gardeners welcome visitors into their oasis and enjoy talking about what they are growing themselves. The program actually helps people grow their own organic veggies at five different greenhouse and garden locations throughout the Resort Municipality of Whistler – the Cheakamus Gardens are just one such site. Growing vegetables nearby reduces the carbon footprint of our food, eliminates packaging, and allows people to learn more about our important connections to local produce. Gardens like the ones in AWARE's GROW program are a great way for locals and visitors to spend time in the great outdoors and take advantage of the physical and mental health benefits associated with fresh veggies.

AWARE is a member-driven charity that works to protect the natural environment in Whistler and the Sea to Sky through advocacy and awareness, while empowering others to do the same through science-based research and education.

Address Jane Lake Road, Whistler, BC V0N 1B1, www.awarewhistler.org,
info@awarewhistler.org | Getting there From the Sea to Sky Highway, exit at Cheakamus
Lake Road, then go over the bridge on Legacy Way, and turn right on Jane Lakes Road. |
Hours Unrestricted | Tip Want to plant some flowers or vegetables before you leave
Whistler? The Whistler Garden Centre in Function Junction can help with the seeds
(1100 Millar Creek Road, www.whistlerflowers.com).

22 The Cheakamus Dam
From powder to power

British Columbia has an abundance of streams and rivers, and the government-owned utility, BC Hydro, operates 82 dams at 40 locations in the province. So if you ever wondered what powers the lifts, lights, and lounges at Whistler, you can go see the Cheakamus Dam, a great example of a typically small BC hydro dam along the Sea to Sky Highway, 25 kilometres (15.5 miles) south of the Village.

The dam feeds into a central grid that in turn powers the entire province – not just Whistler. Many BC Hydro dams generate their electricity from reservoirs, and in 1926, the Daisy Lake Reservoir was created when the Cheakamus Dam was built. That dam was replaced in 1984 with a 29-metre-high (95-foot), earth-filled structure you see today. Water flows 11 kilometres (7 miles) from Daisy Lake and through two penstocks before reaching the 157 megawatt Cheakamus Generating Station on the Squamish River.

Most people driving the Sea to Sky Highway wouldn't even know they're passing 10 other dams not visible from the road. The mountains on the way to Whistler have an abundance of pristine snow and slowly melting icy glaciers running down them and emptying into the ocean. A different and much smaller type of dam is known as a run of river diversion structure. These diversion structures don't create reservoirs but instead divert part of the flowing water to a turbine downstream. About 15 years ago, BC Hydro entered into long-term contracts with independent power producers to build smaller, environmentally friendly and green generating facilities along the Sea to Sky Corridor to help meet the future demand. These run of river dams – with names like Furry Creek, Brandy Wine, and Skookum – generate between 8 and 50 megawatts of power each.

So next time you're skiing, think about how the beautiful, white powder beneath your skis also powers your lift ride up the mountain.

Address Squamish Valley Road, Squamish, BC V0N 1B1 | Getting there Take the Sea to Sky Highway to Squamish Valley Road. | Hours Unrestricted | Tip There is a big, orange bridge on the Sea to Sky Highway 13 kilometres (8 miles) south of the Cheakamus Dam. It's a fortified heavy metal structure, and it's named BOB – short for Big Orange Bridge.

23 _ Cheakamus River Bungee
You'll fall for it

On April Fools' Day, 1979, three members of The Dangerous Sport Club jumped off the 80-metre-high (260-foot-high) Clifton Suspension Bridge in Bristol, England, harnessed in bungee cords to spare them from an otherwise certain death. The first member went down wearing a top hat and tails and holding a bottle of champagne. And thus was modern bungee jumping born! Today, people all over the world bungee jump in all sorts of getups. Some even jump in the nude. What Whistler brings to the table of the adventurous is the added joy of jumping in winter. What could be more Canadian than bungee jumping in a toque above a glacier-fed river covered in snow?

Located just a few minutes south of Whistler Village, the bungee bridge over the Cheakamus River invites you to leap off 50 metres (160 feet) above the glacially fed, icy currents below. For those who love to count the ways to defy death, this is a new, spine-tingling way that you've been dreaming of to get your heart beating overtime. And not only can you jump wearing a toque, you can jump solo, in tandem, and even in a wheelchair.

But if winter is not your scene, fear not! The bridge is open all year round, and you can jump in any season you like. In fact the only time that you can't jump off this bridge is when there's a lightning storm because the bridge is made of metal – that experience would be a bit too electrifying.

For those who like to mix some natural history in with their near-misses, it may interest you to know the river's name is an anglicization of the name of Chiyakmesh, or "People of the Fish Weir," a village of the Squamish people and a reserve of the Squamish Nation. The Cheakamus is a tributary of the Squamish River, which begins on the west slopes of Outlier Peak in Garibaldi Provincial Park, on the southeastern outskirts of Whistler.

Address Calcheak Forest Service Road, Whistler, BC V0N 1B1, +1 (604) 938-9333, www.whistlerbungee.com, bookings@whistlerbungee.com | **Getting there** From the Sea to Sky Highway, take the Cal-Cheak exit and follow the Cal-Cheak Forest Service Road about 3 kilometres (2 miles) to Bungee Bridge. | **Hours** By appointment only | **Tip** If you'd rather just relax and let the others jump, there's a beautiful picnic spot on the far side of the bridge at small and scenic Pothole Lake (possibly named after the access road).

24 The Chief

Canada's tallest granite monolith

Halfway between Vancouver and Whistler, a large granite dome of rock towers 702 metres (2,300 feet) over the nearby town of Squamish. Known colloquially as "The Chief," its proper name is "The Stawamus Chief." But the original name given to it by the Squamish First Nation people is "Siám' Smánit." According to legend, the mountain is an enormous longhouse that was transformed to stone by Xáays (Transformer Brothers). The face of the mountain shows the outlines of the animals and people who were celebrating in this longhouse. The dark black, vertical line is said to have been created by the corrosive skin of Sínulhka, a giant, two-headed sea serpent, when it slithered over the rock face.

Today, the face of The Chief is more likely to be covered by adventurous mountain climbers, who scale its heights from many different approaches. The serious rock climbers will attack The Chief from the slabby routes of The Apron, to the multi-pitch climbs of The Grand Wall, or routes on the north end of The Chief, and up routes with names like "Slot Machine" and "Exasperator." The less adventurous but equally determined can take an intermediate hiking path up to First Peak (1.3 kilometres/535 metres elevation), then carry on to Second Peak (2.4 kilometres/580 metres elevation) and onto Third Peak (3.4 kilometres/702 metres) – if your thighs are not yet on fire. When going for all three peaks, allow 3–5 hours for the round trip. It's worth the effort to see the spectacular views of the Howe Sound and Mount Garibaldi.

The only place in North America where you will find a taller granite monolith is at Yosemite National Park in California, where El Capitán rises 910 metres (3,000 feet) over the western end of Yosemite Valley. Nigeria's Zuma Rock (725 metres/2,378 feet) is close to the same height as The Chief.

Address Approximately 4 kilometres south of Squamish, www.exploresquamish.com/trails-routes/stawamus-chief | **Getting there** Take the Sea to Sky Highway to Stawamus Chief Provincial Park. The main Chief trail starts at a well-marked staircase. Free parking in the park's lot. | **Hours** Unrestricted | **Tip** For a shorter excursion, take the trail to nearby Shannon Falls (www.exploresquamish.com/trails-routes/shannon-falls) or, slightly higher up at Lukas Falls (www.bcparks.ca/explore/parkpgs/shannon).

25 The Cinema 8
Whistler in Hollywood

It's no surprise that Whistler is featured in many films, given that it has the world's most spectacular backdrop at its doorstep. There are also a couple of film festivals that take place every year in the resort that attract thousands of fans and further fuses the relationship between the town and the movie industry. The Cinema 8, Whistler's own little silver screen theatre, where the locals catch the latest Hollywood blockbusters, punches above its weight level and stages many premier screenings and serves as a hub for the competitions.

Think of it as Hollywood North. The stunning, snow-capped mountains and landscapes of the Sea to Sky region make for beautiful sets for movies and TV shows alike. Films you may have seen that feature that incredible scenery include *The Revenant* starring Leonardo DiCaprio and Tom Hardy. It was a western based on the life of a frontiersman who guides a group through unsettled territory. On the other end of the script spectrum was the film *Star Trek Beyond*, which was the third movie in the franchise and followed Captain Kirk and other members of the USS *Enterprise* as they crash-landed on a mysterious planet. *The Twilight Saga*, a series of five movies with vampires and wolves, took advantage of the old-growth forests and foggy weather around Whistler to create an eerie atmosphere.

The Whistler Film Festival takes place in early December and screens over 80 new movies each year. It's been going strong since 2001. Then there's the Whistler Ski and Snowboard Festival that puts a large emphasis on creating short films. The epicentre of much of this activity is the Village 8 Cinema. It's a bit of an anomaly because it only has six screens. But locals love the place because tickets are cheap: $13 for adults, discounted to $8 on Tuesdays. It's a great place to relax with a big bag of popcorn and some candy and watch a movie after a day on the slopes. Just try not to fall asleep in the theatre's comfy seats.

Address 4295 Blackcomb Way, Whistler, BC V8E 0X2, +1 (604) 932-5815, www.cinemaclock.com/theatres/village-8-cinemas-whistler | Getting there From the Sea to Sky Highway, exit onto Lorimer Road and turn left on Blackcomb Way. | Hours See website for movie schedule | Tip Whistler has its very own radio station just around the corner from the Village 8 Cinema, with a glass window to see the studio and announcers (4295 Blackcomb Way, No. 126, www.mountainfm.com).

26 Cloudraker Skybridge

The highest suspension bridge in Canada

Suspension bridges aren't for the faint of heart, and Cloudraker Sky-bridge, with its James Bond-worthy moniker, is no exception. It sways 600 metres (2,000 feet) above the Whistler Bowl. Its cage metal bottom lets you see right through its grates, giving you a completely mind-blowing, 360-degree experience. The bridge is made up of 101 steel modules linked together like a string of pearls, each section weighing 228 kgs (500 lbs). They connect Whistler Peak and its West Ridge on four cables, each one tensioned to over 36,000 kgs (80,000 lbs).

What on earth would possess anyone to build a suspension bridge in the extreme altitudes at the top of Whistler Mountain, a dizzying 2,240 metres (7,350 feet) above the valley floor? That's easy to answer: the view. There is no better place to admire the famous Black Tusk, an unusually shaped, imposing 2,300-metre (7,608-foot) pinnacle of volcanic rock, and the dozens of other incredible peaks that surround it, than from the spectacular Cloudraker Skybridge. Until the bridge was built in 2018, those breathtaking views were reserved for experienced skiers who could catch glimpses of them from the Peak chairlift. But know this before you go: if it is windy on the day you're crossing the bridge, it will sway.

After overcoming any feelings of acrophobia and having made it from one end of the 130-metre-long (427-foot-long) bridge to the other, you might as well challenge yourself to one more vertigo-inducing experience: the Raven's Eye Cliff Walk. This triangular, metal platform is just a few steps away from the suspension bridge you just crossed. It extends out 12.5 metres (41 feet) and hangs a whopping 50 metres (164 feet) above the ski run below. But this platform is stationary and doesn't sway, so you can take a deep breath and marvel at all the glorious sites around you, including Rainbow Mountain, Alta Lake, and the Valley below.

Address The top of Whistler Mountain, Whistler, BC V0N 1B4, www.whistlerblackcomb.com | Getting there Take the Creekside Gondola or the Village Gondola. | Hours See website for lift schedule | Tip If bridges get you high, take the moderate 8.7-kilometre (5.4 miles) Brandywine Trail Loop hike to the Cal-Cheak Suspension Bridge, starting at the Cal-Cheak Recreation Site (www.sitesandtrailsbc.ca).

27 _ Crazy Canuck Drive

Start your sign-searching safari here

You can learn a lot about the ethos of a town just by looking at its street names. Naturally, some of the names of roads in a world-class mountain resort are whimsically aligned with nature, while others pay tribute to famous local athletes. With so many different kinds of wild animals, interesting birds, and beautiful trees to look at, it should come as no surprise then to see names like Beaver Lane, Eagle Drive, or Aspen Court. Nancy Greene Drive on the other hand pays tribute to Canada's most decorated ski racer (see ch. 4). But what's the story behind Crazy Canuck Drive?

Four young men who trained at Whistler during the 1970s changed the course of modern ski racing forever. This rag-tag group of Canadians were simply known as the "Crazy Canucks," and they earned a global reputation for reckless downhill skiing, combined with courage, risk, and intense teamwork beyond belief. They were Dave Irwin, Dave Murray, Steve Podborski, and Ken Read. These "Kamikaze Canadians" burst onto the World Cup Ski circuit with unheard-of flair and determination, beating the Europeans on their home slopes in a sport they rarely lost to anyone. From 1974 to 1984, the Crazy Canucks won a total of 39 World Cup podiums, including 14 first place finishes. Steve Podborski called their mercurial rise to the top of the World Cup circuit a Cinderella story of continually facing seemingly insurmountable odds. Their success went on to inspire Canada's national ski program and the next generation of young skiers.

Most of the street names at Whistler, like Crazy Canuck Drive, are far more interesting than what you'll find in the city and worth looking into. Plus, it can be fun to drive around and take selfies in front of your favourites. Street names like Needless Road and Drifters Place are well worth the drive. After your sign-searching safari is over you can relax and unwind on Easy Street.

Address Crazy Canuck Drive, Whistler, BC V0N 1B8 | **Getting there** From the Sea to Sky Highway, exit at Crazy Canuck Drive. | **Hours** Unrestricted | **Tip** Want to get your skis tuned up before hitting the slopes in the morning so you can ski like a Crazy Canuck? Can-Ski Creekside offers a handy service where their technicians service your boards overnight while you sleep (220-2051 Lake Placid Road, www.whistlerblackcomb.com).

The Crazy Canucks captured the world's hearts during the 1970s and 80s with their success on the World Cup Circuit and their fearless racing style. In the early 1970s no non-European had ever won a men's World Cup downhill and it wasn't expected to change. The young Canadian racers - Dave Murray, Jim Hunter, Dave Irwin, Ken Read and Steve Podborski - changed all this. In 1975 Ken Read won at Val d'Isere and Canadians began appearing on world cup podiums with increasing regularity.

The Crazy Canucks had close ties to Whistler; Dave Murray was the first racer from Whistler Mountain Ski Club to race in the World Cup. After retiring from racing he ran the Summer Camps on Whistler Mountain for many years. Steve Podborski attended the Whistler Mountain Summer Camps as a teenager.

28 Creekside Brass Plaques

History at your feet

If you're visiting Whistler for a short stay, brushing up on the local history and memorizing key dates may be low on your priority list. You're unlikely to dive into a 500-page book about the resort municipalities' development. The good news, then, is that a quick primer is available to you at the Creekside Village. Whistler's abbreviated – extremely abbreviated – chronological milestones are commemorated on nine brass plaques set into the sidewalk pavers in the local commercial plaza. Each plaque is about one-foot in diameter, and they are spaced about 9–12 metres (30–40 feet) apart.

Finding them is a bit of a treasure hunt in itself. Start at the Southwest side of the plaza on the lower level. You will find the first one not far from the BC Government Liquor store. It celebrates what some people consider to be the most important development of Whistler's early days: the arrival of the Pacific Great Eastern Railway (PGE) in 1914. Stroll 9 metres (30 feet) toward Whistler Mountain, and learn about when Whistler's founder Myrtle Philips opened the Rainbow Lodge and fishing retreet (see ch. 66). Walk a bit further up the slight incline and find the metal plate that focuses on 1930 and the opening of Whistler's first community school. Each plaque shares short little snippets of easily digestible Whistler history. Memorize three or four of them, and you can impress – or bore to tears – the people you share a chairlift ride with later in the day. The brass plaques end with the year 2003 and Whistler's winning the bid to host the 2010 Olympic Winter Games (see ch. 1).

The history of Whistler as we know it today began at Creekside. In February 1966, the mountain officially opened here, with one six-person gondola, the red chairlift, and two T-bars. Whistler Blackcomb now boasts 37 lifts, and Creekside has become the more laid back, family-friendly neighbourhood of the town.

Address 2071 Lake Placid Road, Whistler, BC V6E 0B6 | Getting there From the Sea to Sky Highway, exit at Lake Placid Road. | Hours Unrestricted | Tip One of Whistler's oldest and best-known bars is Dusty's, named after a stuffed former Texas bronco that was brought up to Whistler in the back of a pick-up truck in 1979. The taxidermy horse was a local character until he met his final demise – "Dusty to dust" (2040 London Lane).

29 Cultural Kiosks
Journey of discovery along Highway 99

Driving between Whistler and Vancouver, you'll pass a number of unique roadside kiosks designed in the shape of the traditional cedar bark hats of the Squamish and Lil'Wat First Nations people. There are actually nine kiosks: five on the east side of the highway, two in Whistler, and two on the west side. Together, they reveal a route rich in the mystery and wonder of First Nations' oral history, supernatural beings, and unique place names.

Visiting the kiosks is a great way to learn how mighty Thunderbird, giant two-headed serpents, and other mythical beings have shaped the land. On the way from Vancouver to Whistler, make your first stop at Horseshoe Bay to learn about the two giants who waged an epic battle using slingshots. Then travel 32.2 kilometres (20 miles) to the Britannia Beach kiosk, where trespassers were transformed into stone. Another 8.8 kilometres (5.5 miles) down the road takes you to the Stawamus Chief kiosk, where you will discover where the Squamish Nation medicine people trained. Go another 2.8 kilometres (1.75 miles) to the Adventure Centre kiosk in Squamish and walk the trail left by the serpent Sinulhk-ay. Then travel 40.7 kilometres (25.25 miles) to the Brandywine kiosk, landing place of the great Thunderbird. A final 8.9-kilometres (5.5-mile) drive will take you to the kiosk at Olympic Plaza in Whistler, and just 0.6 kilometres (.37 miles) away is the kiosk at the Squamish Lil'Wat Cultural Centre, an architectural masterpiece.

On the way from Whistler to Vancouver, there are the two additional kiosks. The first, 32.5 kilometres (20 miles) from the Cultural Centre, is the Tantalus kiosk, named for the elite alpine hunters immortalized in the towering granite of the Tantalus Mountains. A further 47 kilometres (29 miles) down the road takes you to the kiosk at Tunnel Point, where you'll experience a stunning view of the Howe Sound. Collectively, the kiosks deliver culture on the go.

Address Between Horseshoe Bay and Whistler, along the Sea to Sky Highway, www.slcc.ca/experience/cultural-journey | **Getting there** All kiosks are on the Sea to Sky Highway. See website for exact locations. | **Hours** Unrestricted | **Tip** The gift shop at the Squamish Lil'Wat Cultural Centre is a great place to view and purchase First Nations art and merchandise (4584 Blackcomb Way, www.slcc.ca/visit/gallery-gift-shop).

30 __ The First Chair Lift
From Mid Station to the Roundhouse

Whizzing up Whistler Mountain on one of the amazing, super-fast, six-person express chair lifts, it's hard to imagine what getting up the same hill was like back in 1966. For those of you inquisitive enough to want to sit in one of the old, slow, rickety chairs, here's the attraction for you. It's one of the original seats that serviced the mountain when it first opened. When you sit on it, please note that it has no safety bar or footrest, plus the room that it provides for one's *derrière* can best be described in one word: cramped.

The Garibaldi Lift Company that owned, developed, and opened Whistler in 1966 rigged that original chair onto the Red Chair lift line. Additionally, in order to open the mountain that year, investments were made in a gondola at Creekside, and two T-bars. That was it. Whistler consisted of a chair lift, two T-bars and a gondola. Today, there are 37 different lifts on the mountain with the capacity to move 100,000 people per hour. That old Red Chair, which was removed from service in 1992, was replaced by the Big Red Express, a safer, faster, and more comfortable ride that traces the exact same route as the old chair from Mid-station to the Roundhouse restaurant.

When the mountain first opened, there was no real cafeteria or food service. During the first winter, staff served hot drinks, soup, and sandwiches off a picnic table, using a gas Coleman camp stove in the aptly named Red Shack, which sat at the top of the Red Chair. The next season, the first Roundhouse was built. It was patterned after a building in California and was designed as a round warming hut with a huge, open fireplace in the middle, where the skiers warmed their feet (hence the name Roundhouse). The new, modern, full-service Roundhouse is a great place to take a break for coffee or lunch. But when you're in the Village, you can sit in the old red chair for a historical Whistler selfie.

Address 4329 Main Street, Whistler, BC V8E 1B2 | **Getting there** From the Sea to Sky Highway, exit onto Village Gate Boulevard and turn left onto Northlands Boulevard, then turn right onto Main Street. Destination is near the library. | **Hours** Unrestricted | **Tip** Ski trail maps are handed out for free at the Guest Services windows in the Whistler Village. After getting your hands on one, it's interesting to trace exactly where the red chair is and how it is connected to the original Creekside Gondola.

31___First It Was a Dump

It was hard to bear

In the days before recycling, discarded grocery waste went to the Whistler Dump. So much food refuse and waste were dropped off there that it became one of the best places in Canada to spot hungry bears, who, of course, were rummaging through it looking for snacks. Many visitors and locals are vaguely aware that where today's beautiful Whistler Village stands, there once was a dump. But very few know that the dump's epicentre in the Village was actually where today's Hilton Hotel and the golf driving range are.

Before Whistler became a municipality, many of the early homesteaders and lodge owners had no centralized place to bring their garbage. At first, they just buried it and burned it, as did most other people of the time. In the 1960s, a centralized location was identified at the base of Whistler Mountain for a town dump. The Alta Lake Ratepayers Association, the governing municipal body at the time, leased the land where the Hilton and the driving range are today, and with the help of the Valleau Logging Company, the same company that moved the Whistler train wreck (see ch. 35), dug the ditches that would receive tons of garbage.

The Valleau Logging Company then donated their equipment, and resident volunteers raked the garbage into the ditches and then covered them up once filled. Families living in the area were assigned weeks when they were on raking duty, but some of them did a lousy job burying and covering it. Bears would get wind of the garbage left on the surface and invade the area. It's disturbing to note that some people visited the dump to shoot them.

Today, the only shots around that area are golf shots that slice and hook off the range. There is no garbage at the golf course, so you won't see any bears there. Whistler's waste management has moved to the Callaghan Valley, and it's a modern facility fenced off from the bears.

Address Hilton Whistler Resort and Spa, 4050 Whistler Way, Whistler, BC V8E 1H9 | Getting there Driving north on the Sea to Sky Highway, take the Whistler Way exit. | Hours Unrestricted | Tip If you're a golfer and you'd like to get some of your bad garbage shots out of your system, then the driving range at the Whistler Golf Club is just the place (4001 Whistler Way, www.whistlergolf.com).

32 Fitzsimmons Covered Bridge

Beauty and the bridge

What's the most Instagrammable picture that you can post from Whistler? Impossible to say because there is so much great scenery, but the Fitzsimmons Creek Covered Bridge would be near the top of the list. Located in the river valley between the Whistler Town Center and the Upper Village, it's the perfect spot to shoot a 14–person wedding party, or to extend your selfie pole for a great shot of yourself.

The bridge gets you across Fitzsimmons Creek, a spectacular waterway that flows down from the mountains. The creek's unique turquoise color is the result of glacial till, the tiny particles of suspended rock that are produced when a massive glacier grinds the Earth's surface for hundreds of thousands of years. The creek, is named after Jimmy Fitzsimmons, who operated a small mine near the head of the creek. He also has a glacier, a mountain, and a chair lift named after him.

True covered bridges are a bit of a rarity. About 1,600 remain in the world. The question you may want to ponder while crossing over Fitzsimmons creek, is just why are covered bridges covered? It's kind of like asking why is the sky blue? *Just because* is not a good enough answer. A covered bridge is actually the technical name for a certain type of structure defined by a timber truss, or frame, which distributes the weight of the load bearing deck. Of course, covering a bridge also shields the trusses and deck from the elements. Since wooden bridges that have exposed superstructures tend to decay from rot, covering and roofing them protects the trusses from the weather, so they last longer.

Bridge engineers and architects state that uncovered wooden bridges have a 20-year lifespan, but if you covered a wooden bridge with a roof, it could last upwards of 100 years. So there is no hurry to get to the Fitzsimmons covered bridge for that selfie. But why wait?

Address South end of Rebagliati Park, 4540 Blackcomb Way, Whistler, BC V0N 1B4 | Getting there From the Sea to Sky Highway, take the Village Gate exit and turn left on Blackcomb Way, then park at first right. | Hours Unrestricted | Tip Not far away is a small pedestrian bridge that connects Olympic Plaza and the Town Plaza. Twenty small bronze art and science objects sit atop both of its side rails. Try and find the microscope.

33 Fitzsimmons Skills Park
Mountain biking Mecca

The all-encompassing, massive Whistler Mountain Bike Park is the most famous and popular bike park in the entire world. A unique and authentic pedal-powered mountain biking culture is alive and well at Whistler from May through till October. It would take days if not weeks to cover the expansive network of bike trails that the mountain offers. It's a mind-boggling network of over 80 kilometres (50 miles) of trails to explore, making it the number one bike park on the planet. And here's the best part: the park is accessible by gondola and chair lift, and it's "gravity fed," meaning that little or no pedaling is required. Gravity does all the work. There is so much to take in, where do you begin? And if you are not into tearing down the mountain and just want to watch some crazies go at it, where can you go?

Fitzsimmons Skills Park is a good place to start. Located near Fitzsimmons Creek, the municipally run multi-acre park provides locals and guests an opportunity to improve skills before taking on the challenges of the aforementioned trails. There are jumps for every level of rider. Beginners can roll the smallest jumps, slowly building confidence before getting some real air under their tires. It's inspiring to watch the more skilled riders hit the big lines. The Skills Park has updated technical and freeride features that guide riders through a series of skills. Plus, the park has great viewing spots to stop and enjoy. It has a water bottle filling station, a bright yellow stationary bike tire pump, and a shared bike tool post too.

With all the great bike trails, cycling infrastructure, and amenities that Whistler has to offer, it should come as no surprise that the biggest annual event that the resort stages every summer focuses on mountain biking. Crankworx, the biggest annual gathering of the mountain biking community in the world, is considered the Super Bowl of the sport well worth attending.

Address 4330 Blackcomb Way, Whistler, BC V0N 1B4, www.whistler.ca/culture-recreation/ facilities/bike-park, resortexperience@whistler.ca | Getting there From the Sea to Sky Highway, take the Village Gate exit and turn left on Blackcomb Way. Park at first right. | Hours Unrestricted | Tip The Top of the World Bike Trail on the peak of Whistler Mountain serves up some of the world's best mountain biking amidst the backdrop of the granite spires of the Coast Mountain Range (www.trailforks.com/trails/top-world).

34__Float Planes Harbour Air
Turning seaplanes into e-planes

In 1982, when Harbour Air first began servicing BC's logging industry with two float planes, there were no such things as environmentally friendly, rechargeable electric lawn mowers, bikes, or cars. Back then, global warming was no big deal, and the thought of a zero emission, all-electric floatplane would have been scoffed at and regarded as a prop in a Gene Roddenberry science-fiction TV series.

Since then, this innovative seaplane operator just keeps on getting greener and greener. In 2007, they became the world's first carbon neutral airline through carbon credit off-setting 100% of the emissions associated with the fuel used by their 40 seaplanes. And then, on December 10, 2019, the airline moved towards going even greener.

That's when, in front of a crowd of aviation enthusiasts in Richmond, BC, Harbour Air staged a successful, 10-minute flight of the world's first all-electric commercial aircraft. On that big day, the company's founder and CEO Greg McDougall flew a six-passenger DHC-2 de Havilland Beaver magnified by a 750-horsepower (560-kW) magni500 propulsion system into the air off of the Fraser River. It was a huge deal reported around the world, with the flight ushering in a new era in aviation – the Electric Age.

Unfortunately though, it will be a while before you can hop on board one of these quiet, green machines to go skiing. The plan now is to convert their entire fleet to electric engines within two years depending upon approvals from transport Canada. It's the short flights, like the one to Whistler that Harbour Air operates today with gas engines that will ultimately make electric planes viable. Harbour Air's scheduled flight from Vancouver to Whistler takes only 45 minutes; perfect for a plug in. Finally, just when you thought it couldn't get any greener, get this. In Whistler, the Airline operates its flights from the pristine waters of Green Lake.

Address 8069 Nicklaus North Boulevard, Whistler, BC V0N 1B0, +1 (604) 932-6615, www.harbourair.com | Getting there Take the Sea to Sky Highway exit at Nicklaus North Boulevard. | Hours See website for schedule | Tip Nearby, about a three-iron shot, from where the float planes land, you'll find Whistler's Best Patio at the Nicklaus North Golf Course (8080 Nicklaus North Boulevard, www.nicklausnorth.com).

35 Forest Train Wreck

Tragedy transformed

Sure, you may have heard about the Whistler train wreck, but have you actually *seen* it? If not, do yourself a favour, and make a point of visiting this unique piece of off-track, accidental history. For one thing, it's a very pleasant hike that just about anyone can enjoy. No expensive hiking equipment needed. The only possibly challenging bit is the suspension bridge you'll need to cross to reach the rail cars, but that challenge is all in the mind – you can do it. But the real thrill, after a 20-minute hike through scenes and smells of greenery, is the startling sight of the metal rail cars strewn around the ancient crash site like so many discarded children's toys.

For the philosophically minded, the site is a living metaphor for the role and impact of man-made technology upon the natural world. Or, since many of the cars have been turned into metal canvases for graffiti artists, perhaps the site is proof that art has the power to overcome tragedy and turn wrecks into wonders. You'll have to see it and experience it to decipher what it all means for you.

For a long time, how the boxcars got there was a bit of a mystery. The derailment happened at a time when few people lived in the area and long before Whistler had a newspaper to record events like this for posterity. When people eventually discovered the collection of boxcars, they also saw that the cars were surrounded by old growth trees in pristine condition. What kind of train wreck leaves surrounding trees undamaged?

It took 60 years for the riddle to be solved, but it eventually came to light that the boxcars came off the rails by accident in 1956, the inevitable result of a train going too fast. A local family with lumber equipment was engaged to move the boxcars away from their original wreck site, and dragged them uphill to their current resting place. And that's where they've been ever since.

Address Whistler Quarry Road, Whistler, BC V0N 1B1 | Getting there From the Sea to Sky Highway, exit onto Cheakamus Lakes Road, then turn right on Legacy Way. Go over the bridge, then turn right on Jane Lakes Road to destination. | Hours Unrestricted | Tip If the trails and rails inspire you to get rolling, check out the bikes at nearby Chromag Bikes (1220 Alpha Lake Road, No. 4, www.chromagbikes.com).

36 Forged Axe

You haft-a try it

Is there anything more backcountry, more outdoorsy, more Whistlery, or more Canadian than recreational axe throwing? Historians say the sport of axe throwing can be traced back thousands of years. This relies on the – probably true – theory that humans throughout history have always derived great pleasure from throwing sharp objects at trees, walls, targets, and other things.

Setting aside all the legacy of Vikings, medieval armies, and the utility of the tomahawk, the modern version of axe throwing owes a great debt to the timber sports and lumberjacking competitions that thrive in places like the Sea to Sky corridor, where the lumber tradition runs strong. On an organized sport basis, its modern history can be traced to the Backyard Axe Throwing League (BATL), which was started in Toronto, far across the country from Whistler, in 2006. That league led to formation of the National Axe Throwing Federation (NATF) in 2016, which morphed into the International Axe Throwing League (IATL) in 2019, which now has members on four continents and 85 cities. Not to be outdone, the World Axe Throwing League (WATL) was started in 2017 and boasts membership from 19 axe throwing nations. You get the picture: this is a hot new organized sport, and you should probably find out what it's all about. So you may want to pick up an axe and learn a few key skills yourself.

Forged Axe, at this location since 2017, was inspired by a backwoods rafting trip on the Chilko River. So you know it has honest roots – no big corporate scheme here. The friendly, experienced coaches will give you the safety rules and teach you the basics, from one-handed throws to two-handed, from hatchet-style to the longer style axe, and will introduce you to some axe throwing games. If you've ever played darts or gone curling, you're halfway there. You must wear closed-toe shoes, but there's no other gear required.

Address 1208 Alpha Lake Road, Whistler, BC V0N 1B1, +1 (778) 770-2240, www.forgedaxe.ca | Getting there From the Sea to Sky Highway, exit at Alpha Lake Road/ Function Junction. | Hours See website for hours | Tip The boutique craft brewery Coast Mountain is located next door and well worth a visit after the axe throwing – not before! (1212 Alpha Lake Road, No. 2, www.coastmountainbrewing.com).

37 __ Fresh St. Market Cowbells

You'll be moo-ved

Grocery shopping will eventually end up on your list of things to do at Whistler. There are half a dozen small supermarkets in the Resort Municipality that are all good. But one of them, the Fresh St. Market, which is the largest and newest, has made a real effort to create a unique and memorable Whistler experience while you fill your cart.

Look for a massive mural of outdoor adventure photos shot by locals and store employees and a totally cool display of hundreds of old skis and snowshoes from around BC pinned to a 40-foot wall. And the produce section features wheelbarrows full of in-season vegetables grown by BC farmers in the nearby Pemberton Valley. All of these sites will help you realize you've left the big city behind. There's even a section of the store dedicated to the fine art of packing your own lunch to eat later when you're taking a break on the mountain. There's another section packed with winter accessories, like toques, mitts, and windshield scrapers for the winter and inner tubes, ice coolers, and suntan lotion for the summer. The Shed Café in the store serves organic coffee from the Whistler Roasting Company. Many items at Fresh St. Market are locally sourced.

Look up when you get to the dairy section. There's a massive display of cowbells, all carefully placed together to spell out that old familiar sound that Bessie makes. And not far from there is a collection of 14 dairy urns, the tall cylindrical containers used for the transportation of milk. They were collected from farms around the Fraser Valley, the fertile lands to the south.

Also in the dairy section is Whistler's best cheese selection: specialty cheeses from local makers, round cheeses from around the world, raclettes, farmer's cheeses, unpasteurized cheese, and raw milk cheese. You'll try many interesting cheeses from interesting places, each with a story – and a flavor – all its own.

Address 4330 Northland Boulevard, Whistler, BC V0N 1B4, +1 (604) 938-2850, www.freshstmarket.com/contact/whistler, ithink@freshstmarket.com | Getting there From the Sea to Sky Highway, exit onto Lorimer Road. Just past the intersection, turn right and park at the south end of the Marketplace Shopping Centre. | Hours Daily 8am–9pm | Tip If you like your cheese hot, try the cheese fondue at Crêpe Montagne (4368 Main Street, No. 116, www.crepemontagne.com).

38_ Gord Harder's Fridge
Sticker-studded wonder in Whistler Museum

Whistler Mountain's alpine caretaker Gord Harder got into the habit of putting stickers on his fridge. He started in the 1960s and carried on for nearly 40 years. By the time he was done, the fridge was covered from tip-to-toe with a collection of colourful stickers that reflected and immortalized the culture and ethos of Whistler during its transformation from backcountry home for wandering ski bums, hippies, and adventurers, to one of the world's best-known and loved luxury destinations. It's a fridge you won't want to miss. And, luckily for you, it is just one of several really 'cool' and noteworthy exhibits featured in the cozy and sentimental Whistler Museum.

Wandering through the museum's maze-like series of displays and exhibits, you'll find Olympic and Paralympic paraphernalia. You can pose for a photo with one of the torches used in the 2010 Torch Relay. You'll see an original, 1965-era gondola car from the first gondola in British Columbia during the resort's early days. There is a colorful selection of old-time skis and snowboards, and stories and artefacts about mountain biking. You'll also find information about local real estate development. You'll learn the stories about the people who work on the mountain. There are several interesting audio/video displays, and there's also a display about local landscape artist Chili Thom. You can take a gander at Myrtle Phillip's vintage camp jodhpurs (see ch. 39), along with other artefacts from Rainbow Lodge (see ch. 66). For the aspiring naturalist, there are displays on the local flora and fauna, including a stuffed marmot, the creature responsible for giving Whistler its name (see ch. 110).

The museum was founded as a charitable non-profit society in 1986 by local teacher Florence Petersen. The park nearby is named for her. The museum also hosts seminars and interactive activities throughout the year that are open to locals and visitors alike.

Address 4333 Main Street, Whistler, BC V8E 1B3, +1 (604) 932-2019, www.whistlermuseum.org, info@whistlermuseum.org | Getting there From the Sea to Sky Highway, exit onto Village Gate Boulevard and turn left onto Northlands Boulevard, then turn right onto Main Street. | Hours Mon, Tue, Fri–Sun 11am–5pm, Thu 11am–9pm | Tip Take a short walk over to Whoola Toys Store, where you can pick up toys for kids, and puzzles and games for the whole family to enjoy together (4359 Main Street, www.whoolatoys.ca).

39 — Grave of Myrtle Philip
Resting place of Whistler's First Lady

If you really want to learn about a place, visit its cemetery to see where and how past residents are laid to rest. From Highgate Cemetery in London to Calvary Cemetery in New York, cemeteries tell a lot about a place. The Whistler Cemetery is no exception. Located just a short distance from Rainbow Park, this rugged, three-acre cemetery, in true Whistler fashion, is completely surrounded by forest and located near a mountain bike trail.

The cemetery's oldest memorial tablets were all placed flat so as not to detract from the area's natural landscape. But a new stone columbarium, an above-ground structure designed to hold cremated remains, tastefully manages to fit in with the natural environment. Like the town, the cemetery itself is relatively young (no Victorian poets are buried here), dating back only to 1986. The entrance features a spectacular wooden arch commissioned by one Marlene Lowry to honour the passing of her husband David.

One of the cemetery's most famous residents is Myrtle Philip, known as the First Lady of Whistler. Myrtle first came to the Whistler Valley in 1911 with her husband Alex, and they opened the Rainbow Lodge in 1914 (see ch. 66). In those days, they had to take a boat to Squamish and then hike the rest of the way with pack horses. Over the next 30 years, their success at Rainbow Lodge helped turn Alta Lake into a summer destination. They were, unbeknownst to themselves, largely responsible for creating what would later become the resort municipality of Whistler (see ch. 62).

When the pair sold the lodge in 1948, they had planned to move on, but, like many who came after them, they never quite left. Today Myrtle's name is immortalized in places like The Myrtle Philip Community Centre, the Myrtle Philip Community School, and the "Myrtle Philip Award" presented for academic excellence.

Address Alta Lake Road, Whistler, BC V0N 1B3 | **Getting there** From the Sea to Sky Highway, take the Alta Lake Road exit for 6 kilometres (3.7 miles) to cemetery entrance. Enter the graveyard and walk to the left. | **Hours** Unrestricted | **Tip** Look for other Whistler legends who are buried nearby, including "Crazy Canuck" Dave Murray and trail-blazer Seppo Manniken.

40 Hadaway House

You only live nice

If a James Bond movie is ever filmed in Whistler, this home surely has to be in it. The home's visually arresting architectural style is reminiscent of the now-famous Elrod House used in the 1971 Bond flick *Diamonds Are Forever*. As with the Elrod House, designed by architect John Lautner, this Whistler valley hideaway has retained and embraced many of the natural features in the area and offers its occupants a stunning view of the valley below. Vancouver-based Patkau Architects combined glass, concrete, steel and timber to unfold this shimmering chalet that bedazzles all who see it.

You may become star-struck by looking at the home's glamorous exterior, but don't be fooled into thinking there's nothing substantial going on behind it. The home's casual elegance and sophistication betrays the complexity of its design. Like the Savile Row tailor who makes James Bond's three-piece suits, the Patkau team had to create a truly bespoke home that would fit the client. But, in this case, the inspiration was not Sean Connery's award-winning "Mr. Universe" body. The idea for this home was a wedge-shaped lot stuck between craggy boulders on a slope, and with a full range of building restrictions governing height and overall footprint. It posed no easy challenge.

But Patkau came through like the gadget masters of MI5's Q Division and delivered something truly spectacular. Not only does this 465-square-metre (5,000-square-foot) home fit on the lot precisely, it's designed in such a way that the snow falls off the roof and lands in a very specific place. They even considered how to use the thermal mass of the concrete to dampen temperature swings within the house in summer and winter months.

This home hasn't won an Oscar yet, but its design did win a Canadian Architect Award of Excellence in 2008. And the sight of it is guaranteed to leave you stirred, not shaken.

Address 3801 Sunridge Place, Whistler, BC V0N 1B3, www.patkau.ca/projects/hadaway-house | Getting there From the Sea to Sky Highway, take the Panorama Ridge exit, then turn at the second left onto Sunridge Drive. The destination will be on your right. | Hours Unrestricted from the outside only | Tip For a different kind of Bonding experience, visit nearby Brio Park. It has a tennis court that also includes pickleball lines! Access Brio Park where the Sea to Sky Highway meets the Panorama Ridge road (6 Panorama Ridge, www.whistler.ca/culture-recreation/parks/neighborhood-parks).

41__ Haunted Creekside Building

Who ya gonna call?

You may get a strange, eerie sensation as you walk by or into one of the oldest public buildings in Whistler – the feeling that you are not alone. For the last 40 years, locals have reported numerous frightening encounters and scary sightings in the Whistler Creek area. But it is the building that today houses Creek Bread Wood Fired Pizza, Whistler Creek Lodge, and Whistler Gym that seems to be Ghost Central.

Over the years, there have been too many supernatural occurrences to dismiss the outlandish notion that the building is haunted. For instance, many of the residents that used to live in the hotel year-round reported actually seeing a ghostly figure standing in the corner of their rooms. Hotel staff members once saw a man walking down the hall, then turning, and disappearing into an area with no exits. And cleaners doing the overnight shift can't explain why, with no existing drafts, doors inside the building slowly swing open with a creepy-creaking sound for no apparent reason.

Folklore surrounds the building with explanations. Some say one of the ghosts is a miner or logger named Bill. Then there are accounts from customers gazing up and seeing a ghostly mother and daughter perched in the rafters, with their ghoulish legs dangling as they watched people dining below.

According to the 2012 article in *The Whistler Question,* when Creek-bread's co-owner Jay Gould was preparing for his new restaurant's grand opening in 2009, he saw something that he was "initially reluctant to share. 'It was dark, I was looking out into the room and I saw a women (sic) in white go from the middle of the room and out the doors that lead to the patio. She was high up, maybe ten feet in the air.'" So do visit, but keep your eyes open.

Signs visible in the image:

NO
CREEKBREAD
PARKING
PAST THIS POINT

VIOLATORS WILL BE
TOWED AT
OWNERS EXPENSE

creekbread
&
Gym
PARKING
ONLY
←
All unauthorize
vehicles towe
at owners expe

Address 2021 Karen Crescent, Whistler, BC V0N 1B2 | Getting there From the Sea to Sky Highway, take the Lake Placid Road exit, then turn right onto Karen Crescent. | Hours Unrestricted from the outside | Tip Creekbread Pizza which is in the building, has amazing food. Try the Pemberton Potato Pizza. And don't forget to look up between bites (2021 Karen Crescent, www.creekbread.com).

42 House Rock Memorials

Remembrances in stone

Whistler has long been a magnet to many outdoor enthusiasts and adventurers. People from across Canada and all over the world have made their home here in order to ski, climb, hike, bike, and kayak the mountains, trails, and rivers that are as bewitching as they are abundant. These adventurers have an unquenchable thirst for life, which pushes them forward and challenges them to reach new limits – physical and spiritual. They also form strong bonds of friendship with like-minded individuals and gain respect and admiration from others inspired by their bold acts and outgoing personalities. So when we lose these champions of outdoor adventure, we want to find a meaningful way to remember them. And that's why there is a very unique memorial at House Rock on the Cheakamus River.

The origins of the House Rock memorial extend back to 1988, when local resident Kim Wetaski died rescuing her boyfriend from the rapids at Nairn Falls. Her friends knew she loved this special place along the Cheakamus River, so they scattered her ashes here rather than interring them at the Whistler Cemetery (see ch. 39). They also attached a granite marker in her memory on the rock face.

In the following years, members of the tight-knit community of adventurers have added more memorial plaques, provided by the Whistler Kayak Club and sand-blasted by local sign-maker Charlie Doyle. If you continue along the Riverside Trail which brought you here, you will eventually cross the river at a suspension bridge, and you can take the Farside Trail back down the east side of the river to complete what is known as the Riverside Loop. Altogether it's a pleasant 4.5-kilometre (2.8-mile) hike that takes about two hours to complete. The granite plaques blend in with the local rock face – they are not easy to see unless you're looking for them. And keep a lookout for woodpeckers, whiskey jacks, blue jays, owls, eagles, marmots – and bears.

Address Cheakamus Lake Road | **Getting there** About 8 kilometres (5 miles) south of Whistler Village, turn left onto Cheakamus Lake Road. Go to the left at the fork and over the Cheakamus Lake Road bridge. Park at the parking area on your immediate left. Follow the Riverside Trailhead for about two or three minutes with the river on your left; look for a path down to the river. | **Hours** Unrestricted | **Tip** The trail to Cheakamus Lake starts at the end of Cheakamus Lake Road – a short 7 kilometres (4.5 miles) away (www.trailforks.com/trails/cheakamus-lake-trail).

43 Husky Gas Station
Whistler's seminal gas station

There was no texting, no cell phones, and no Facebook Messenger back in the day. If you were up at Whistler and had to contact someone, one of the only reliable methods of communicating was a tattered and worn bulletin board hanging on the side of the Husky Gas station. Notes scribbled on blue-lined scrap paper with messages like, "Bill we decided not to ski today. Meet us at Dusty's at noon!" were plentifully tacked onto that board. But the Husky served as more than a crude communications hub. It was the landmark where you turned right to get into the old gravel parking lot to go skiing. It had one of the only public washrooms at Whistler. It was the building where you'd quickly run inside and get warmed up after hitch-hiking on the corner for an hour. And yes, they pumped gas too.

The Husky has been there forever, so it seems. It's hard to believe one of the most popular ski resorts in the world, that relies on people being able to drive there and gets over two million visitors per year, got by with only one gas station with a mere eight petrol pumps. Finally, in 2016, a second station, a Chevron, opened in the Whistler Rainbow area. Both stations usually have serious line-ups on Sundays at around 4pm, when the skiers return to Vancouver.

But this unlikely landmark actually holds more history than you could ever imagine. Its very existence was an important contributing factor in the development and growth of Whistler from a small mountain town to an international ski resort in a relatively short period of time. So it's worth paying it a visit to imagine what was only possible because drivers from Vancouver could fill up their gas tanks here.

Today's Husky has a big, clean, and bright convenience store out front and a car wash out back. The washrooms are indoors and although there is no message board hanging on the wall, believe it or not, there is still a pay phone across the street.

Address 2101 Lake Placid Road, Whistler, BC V0N 1B2, +1 (604) 932-3959, www.myhusky.ca | **Getting there** From the Sea to Sky Highway, exit at Lake Placid Road. The destination is right at the intersection. | **Hours** Open 24 hours | **Tip** Roland's Creekside Beer and Wine Store is within walking distance. It's conveniently open seven days a week until 11pm (2129 Lake Placid Road, www.rolandswhistler.com).

44 The Ice Room

The world's coldest vodka-tasting room

If you like to do Arnold Schwarzenegger impersonations, this is the ideal place to try out his corniest lines from the *Batman and Robin* movie in which he played the notoriously chilly villain, Mr. Freeze. At -29°C (-20°F), where else than the coldest vodka-tasting room in the world would be a better place to say, in a deep Austrian accent, "Cool paaahty"? This bar is very cold and very cool.

You'll find the icy Ketel One Ice Room inside the Bearfoot Bistro, a place that once held the Guinness World Record for opening the most bottles of Dom Perignon champagne with a sabre. The Ice Room, formerly a cigar room, first opened in February 2010, just in time for the 2010 Winter Olympics. Many of its first visitors were Olympic athletes. Inside, you will find only vodka. In fact, they serve over 50 different brands from around the world. There are vodkas from places you'd expect, like Russia, Sweden, and Poland, but also from places that might surprise you, like France, New Zealand, and Kazakhstan. Canadian vodkas are well-represented and include several from British Columbia, including Long Table, Deep Cove, Unruly, Schramm (see ch. 74), and Phrog. Many bottles are tantalizingly frozen within the sheets of ice that form the rooms' walls. Each tasting begins with a sample of Ketel One vodka. "Ketel" is the Dutch word for pot (kettle) and in this case is a reference to the traditional brass pots used in the distilling process.

Ketel One vodka was created in 1983 by Carolus Nolet, a tenth-generation descendant of Dutch distiller Joannes Nolet and a big fan of the Bearfoot Bistro. The Ice Room is small, and the Arctic Expedition parka you will be provided with is also cosy, so this is the best opportunity you're going to get to test the theory that vodka is best consumed near its freezing point. But don't let your dedication to scientific experiments linger too long because it really is cold!

Address 4121 Village Green, Whistler, BC V0N 1B4, +1 (604) 932-3433, www.bearfootbistro.com | **Getting there** From the Sea to Sky Highway, exit onto Village Gate Boulevard and turn right at the first set of lights. Stay right onto Whistler Way to the destination on the left. | **Hours** Mon–Thu 2–10pm, Fri–Sun 1–10pm | **Tip** The Whistler Golf Club's driving range is just across the street. The best practise range in town also has club rentals (4001 Whistler Way, www.whistlergolf.com/range).

45 Indigenous Sign Language

An important language to preserve

The green highway signs between Vancouver and Whistler are bilingual, and it is important to know a bit about their origin and background. Prior to the 2010 Olympic Games, all of the road markers were updated to include the traditional names of places along the way in the Squamish language.

Squamish is a Coast Salish language spoken by the Squamish people of the region. The language, which in 1990 was declared by the Chief and Council of the Squamish people to be their official language, is very rare. The First People's Heritage, Language and Cultural Council stated that the language is "critically endangered" and "nearly extinct." In 2010, there were just 10 fluent speakers. Fortunately, the situation has improved since then, and today there are over 400 active learners of the language. In 2014, Capilano University created a Squamish-language program. Simon Fraser University also has a Squamish Language Academy, where students study the language for two years. Both programs increase the number of active learners each year. An English-Squamish dictionary was developed in 2011 to help preserve the language, which historically has been oral and not written.

One idiosyncrasy of the Squamish language that most people pick up immediately when they view the highway signs is the use of a symbol that looks like the number 7. Even experienced linguists can have trouble discerning it. The 7 symbol represents a brief pause or stop in the Squamish language. In phonetics, this is referred to as a glottal stop; think of it as a hyphen. The glottal stop also implies that the consonant in the word is pronounced with a harder emphasis.

Now that you understand that the word Squamish is a loose and mispronounced English adaptation of the word Skwxwú7mesh, you may wonder what the word actually means: a Squamish is a strong and often violent wind along the fjords of the area.

Address Sea to Sky Highway | **Getting there** Signs are posted on the Sea to Sky Highway most of the way between Horseshoe Bay and Whistler. | **Hours** Unrestricted | **Tip** Here's a driving game for you. Since you have an affinity for the number 111, look for the distance marker that identifies the distance to Whistler and Vancouver as 111 kilometres away. What a coincidence that in both directions the number 111 is used as the unit of measurement on the green provincial highway signs.

46   The Interpretive Forest
Is that a Douglas fir?

The best way to experience trees truly is to stand right next to them, up close. Reading about them just doesn't cut it. You have to smell them, feel them, hear them, and see them. You'll see plenty of trees at Whistler, and the Whistler Interpretive Forest is a great place to learn a bit more about them.

The 3,000-hectare (7,400-acre) Interpretive Forest was created in 1980 as a joint undertaking between the Whistler Municipality and the BC Ministry of Forests. This only makes sense when you consider that so much of Whistler's history is rooted in logging, and that forestry is the province's largest manufacturing sector. Don't be intimidated by the size of the forest. You can hike along tree-lined trails for hours and hours if you want, or you can just get out of your car and do the Discovery Trail across from the parking lot, a 300-metre (330-yard), mini-loop walk packed with informative interpretive signs that explain everything you need to know to get you going.

You will learn the difference between a Sitka spruce and Douglas maple – and you'll become familiar with dozens of other tree species. The small signs staked into the ground along the even, soft trail are full of interesting tree facts. For instance, you may already have a small souvenir from Whistler waiting for you at home on your kitchen counter. The common black cottonwood tree, which lives along Whistler's many river banks, gravel bars, and low-lying areas, is harvested for its fibre and then processed into paper towels.

Once you have done the small loop and gotten your fill of silviculture, it's easy to venture further afield for some real hiking in the woods. There are plenty of options from the main parking lot. The mellow, two- to three-hour hike out to the suspension bridge is one of the most popular trails. It's named after Don MacLaurin, a local forester who designed and mapped the area.

Address 1011 BC-99 Whistler, BC V0N 0A0, www.alltrails.com/parks/canada/british-columbia/whistler-interpretive-forest | Getting there From the Sea to Sky Highway, take the Cheakamus Lake Road exit. | Hours Unrestricted | Tip Take some food with you before venturing into the forest. Nearby is the Cebu De Oro Mini Grocery Store. In addition to everything else you'd expect in a neighborhood store, it has some great Filipino snacks (1040 Legacy Way, No. 20, www.cebudeoroservices.biz).

47 Inukshuks of Whistler

More plentiful than you thought

You might have heard about or seen a picture of this awe-inspiring *Whistler Inukshuk.* The image most people think of as "the" Inukshuk here is the one at the top of Whistler Mountain. It has been featured in Olympic communications and seen in other promotional campaigns around the world. But there are in fact six large inukshuks, the stone structures that resemble a giant human, in and around Whistler.

At the entrance to Whistler Village, along Village Gate Boulevard, you'll find another substantial inukshuk. The Resort Municipality of Whistler commissioned Squamish-based Métis artist Moses Peech to create this 5.2-metres (17-foot), 19,500-kg (21.5-ton) figure to let visitors know, in no uncertain terms, that they've arrived at the right place. Since the ancient human-shaped rock sculptures were originally used in the Canadian arctic as navigational aids for travelers on a long trek across the barren landscape, their use today as welcoming destination markers is entirely appropriate.

You can find a third inukshuk at the top of the Peak Chair on Whistler Mountain. There is a fourth one at the top of the 7th Heaven Chair on Blackcomb. A fifth stands near the base of the ski jumps at Whistler Olympic Park, in the nearby Callaghan Valley, and a sixth one is outside the Whistler Public Library. That last one was created by Inuit children at the former Games Information building (where the Olympic Rings now stand at Whistler Olympic Plaza).

The Whistler inukshuks are probably the most photographed in Canada – although the one overlooking English Bay in Vancouver is surely also a strong contender. It was created by Alvin Kanak – artist, hunter, fisher, trapper – based on the Inuit model for the NWT Pavilion at Expo '86. Little did they know that, 20 years later, the design would unite a community from sea to sky and a country from coast to coast to coast.

Address The inukshuk at the entrance to Whistler Village is at the intersection of Village Gate Boulevard and Gateway Drive, Whistler, BC V0N 1B4 | Getting there Varies | Hours Unrestricted | Tip If art carved from stone gets your rocks off, visit Fathom Stone Art for some options that are easier to carry home than a 20 tonne inuksuk (4090 Whistler Way, No. 110, www.fathomstone.com).

48__Journeyman Lodge
The unplugged winter wonderland

The closest any vehicle can get to Journeyman Lodge is 14 kilometres (8.5 miles) from the front door – that's how far away the parking lot is. To experience the Journeyman Lodge, you have to drop your car off at the Callaghan Valley's Alexander Falls base camp and then strap on your cross-country skis and ski in. Or you can strap on your snowshoes and snowshoe in. Either way, dress in layers and plan to spend about four hours to journey up the 13.8-kilometre (8.5-mile) trail. At the end of your trek, you'll be rewarded with the serenity and sensations that made this spot one of the stunning romantic backdrops to *The Bachelor* TV series. Don't plan on spending any time online, as there's no cell phone coverage at the lodge, and no wi-fi either. In fact, the whole area is a non-motorized zone.

The Journeyman Lodge is one of those whimsically magical places, like so many in Whistler, that began with a ski enthusiast standing on top of a mountain, looking around the stunning views unfolding before him, and thinking: "This would be an excellent place for a lodge!" That was 1978. The skier, Nick Slater, collaborated with long-time friend Brad Sills, and together they pushed the project forward.

It took years to achieve the dream, but achieve it they did. And today, it's yours to enjoy: a Canadian ski lodge, with classic Scandinavian design, and artwork supplied by Art Junction (see ch. 7), plonked down among 9,000 hectares (22,250 acres) of winter wonderland and at least 6 kilometres (3.75 miles) of groomed cross-country ski trails right outside the front door.

Snowshoers make their own trails … and you can also make a trail directly to the wood-fired sauna, and follow that up with a refreshing dip in the nearby mountain-fed creek. At the end of the day, look up at a sky unpolluted by city lights. You'll see the stars as clearly as they were seen in centuries past, before motors, wi-fi, and cell phones.

Address Callaghan Valley Road, No. 4, Whistler, BC V0N 1B0, +1 (604) 938-0616, www.callaghancountry.com | Getting there From the Sea to Sky Highway, exit onto Callaghan Road for 10 kilometres (6 miles), and park at the Alexander Falls Touring Centre. Ski or snowshoe from there. | Hours Check website for seasonal openings | Tip There's no bar at the Lodge, but Blackcomb Liquor Store has some options to drop into your backpack (4573 Chateau Boulevard, www.blackcombliquorstore.com).

49 Largest Fleet of Snowcats
Operated by farmers and artists

Operating the snowcats that groom Whistler and Blackcomb's expansive 485 hectares (1,200 acres) of terrain takes a certain kind of temperament, skill set, and background. Resumés with farming experience rise to the top of the pile because ploughing fields and driving giant combine harvesters is similar to grooming slopes, sort of. Artists have an edge too, since it's a very creative vocation. Good grooming, no pun intended, is an art and a science. All groomers have one thing in common though: their passion for the job. And they are in demand at Whistler Mountain. It takes an army of dedicated men and women to sit behind the joystick of North America's largest fleet of snowcats.

There are 38 of these vehicles, to be exact, and they are worth about half a million dollars each. They are all made by a company with a very interesting name, PistenBully. Most of the snowcats are red, but that's where the similarity ends. Some are big, some are smaller. The winch cats require anchoring to make it up steep pitches, and the park cats are specially designed for park and building maintenance. As with all jobs, operating a snowcat has its pluses and minuses. On the plus side would be the amazing moon-lit views and the thrill of having an entire mountainside to yourself. On the minus side are the hours. The graveyard schedule isn't for everyone, and shifts are 10 hours long, so long that before the snowcats head out, they require filling up with 260 liters (68 gallons) of fuel. The snowcats, like their drivers, are nocturnal creatures. They work hard all night and lay idle during the day, when skiers enjoy the fruits of their labors.

Groomers don't have to worry about running out of gas with tanks that large, or about running out of snow to tame for that matter. At Whistler, snow is measured in metres, not centimetres. The resort gets mountains of the stuff: the 10-year average is 11.7 metres (38 feet) of snow each winter!

Address The top of Whistler Mountain, Whistler, BC V0N 1B4, www.whistlerblackcomb.com |
Getting there Take the Creekside Gondola or the Village Gondola. The fleet of snowcats is
parked 300 metres (325 yards) from the roundhouse. | Hours See website for seasonal gondola
hours | Tip Between the snowcats and the Roundhouse sits a strange looking gondola car
designed by General Motors. They took a small gondola and added a truck's grille headlights
and bumpers to it. Why? Who cares; it's worth checking out.

50 Leaning Tree of Nita Lake

Roots and rocks, but no Reggae

The famous town of Pisa, Italy has its leaning tower. Whistler, Canada has its leaning tree. Although not as well-known, the leaning tree on the shores of Nita Lake is well worth the visit.

On the short walk to the tree, you'll pass a forest of beautiful, vertical trees. Hundreds of locals and tourists pass under the leaning tree every day, and the more inquisitive ones must wonder about a couple of things. First of all, how can a tree grow out of a rock? And why is it leaning? It is not that uncommon for there to be a bit of decomposed matter sitting on a rock, or enough dirt in a small wedge for a seedling to get started. As that seedling grows, its roots usually seek out deeper dirt somewhere nearby to give it a solid rooting. This same natural process of a seed finding a place to grow also frequently happens on old stumps or logs, which are then referred to as "nurse logs." There is no such thing as a "nurse rock," but if there was, this one would be a text-book example. Maybe it's the first of its kind.

As the roots grow, they sometimes break fissures in the rock contributing to its breakdown, part of the whole cycle of nature. Eventually, the roots of the leaning tree of Nita Lake took hold on its "nurse rock." The reason that the tree is leaning so much is that, for the first few years of its growth, the roots were not embedded deeply enough to hold it solidly. With its weak root foundation, the tree simply started to lean over. As the years went by and the roots grew deeper into the dirt around the rock, the tree started to slowly grow up more vertically like it should have from the start.

The tree, by the way, is a Douglas fir. It's a common West Coast tree, noted for the huge size it grows to when it matures. from 6.5–28 metres (70–300 feet) tall. They usually grow for about 500 years and can live for up to 1,000 years. So although the leaning tree at Nita Lake is well worth seeing, there is no rush.

Address The tree is located on the east side of Nita Lake. | Getting there From the Sea to Sky Highway, exit at lake Placid Road. Park and find the trail at Creekside Village. | Hours Unrestricted | Tip Nita Lake is a great place to go fly fishing in the summertime. In the winter, it is a great place to go ice fishing. Check to make sure the ice is thick enough before heading out. Don't stand under the leaning tree in a windstorm.

51 Legendary UBC Ski Cabin
It's still there

It was tough for UBC students belonging to the Varsity Outdoor Club (VOC) in the 1960s to complete their degrees. With the incredible skiing the newly opened mountain offered, combined with the wild partying that took place at a brand new ski cabin the students helped build, who had time to study?

The story of how the 40-bed cabin was originally built, the ensuing squabble between the club and the school, and how after the Olympics the run-down property was sold and converted into a modern lodge is worth telling. Hard as it is to believe, when Whistler Mountain developed in the early 1960s, it offered free land to local ski clubs. UBC's Varsity Outdoor Club was a deserving and logical recipient, having promoted outdoor adventure and skiing since its inception in 1917. Legend has it that a graduate student named Karl Ricker organized a group of volunteers to build the structure that still stands today.

Their first hurdle, as they enthusiastically arrived with compasses and measuring tapes in hand, was simply to find the rectangular piece of donated land in the middle of nowhere. Working when classes weren't in session and sleeping on site in a big tent, the young crew finished the cabin in 1965 for about $16,000 in materials. Youthful enthusiasm resulted in it actually opening before the lifts began operating. The Vancouver *Province* ran the headline, "Students Get An A For Effort."

By 1974, however, the cabin was under-used by the VOC, partly because many of their members now went cross-country skiing at other locations. Unfortunately, years of litigation followed. The legendary partying continued for decades after that until the cabin slowly withered away. In 2013, the UBC Alma Mater Society held a referendum, and the property was sold and converted into a lodge. Today, it is the Whistler Lodge Hostel and open to the public. And its original spirit remains.

Address 2124 Nordic Drive, Whistler, BC V8E 0A6, +1 (604) 932-6604, www.whistlerlodgehostel.com | Getting there Heading north on the Sea to Sky Highway, exit onto Nordic Drive. Follow road to destination. | Hours Unrestricted from the outside, except for hostel guests | Tip At the bottom of Nordic Drive, there is a foot bridge that crosses the highway and leads to the Valley Trail. It's a fortified metal structure that has some of the fencing on its sides installed in a clever art deco pattern.

52 Library Living Room
Read a book by the fire in the library

You know those huge sprawling mansions and expensive PRIVATE chalets you see all over Whistler – the ones you are unlikely ever to be invited into (see ch. 103)? They all have spacious living rooms, huge plate glass windows, timber frame beams, beautiful mountain views, cozy fireplaces, and comfy chairs to sink into and immerse yourself in a good book. Hey, wait a minute – that's the Whistler Public Library, and as the word "public" implies, everyone is welcome. Only in a special place like Whistler would you find a library with a big fireplace. And the Whistler Public Library is just as well appointed and decorated as any of those expensive abodes on the hill. You can be guaranteed that they have more books to read there than any private home too.

When you sit in what is often referred to by the locals as "Whistler's Living Room," it's hard to imagine it all began as a small book collection in the 130-square-metre (1,400-square-foot) basement of the Municipal Hall in 1986, when the local Rotary club donated the books and materials required to open the resort's first library. Back then, they only had 4,600 brand new books and 380 library cardholders. Fast-forward to today, when 150,000 books grace the shelves, and there are 5,760 library cardholders.

Today, the popular, beautiful, ultra-modern, 1,115-square-metre (12,000-square-foot) library gets about 250,000 visits a year, consisting of locals, weekend homeowners, and visitors from around the world. If you quietly wander into the section with books and magazines on architecture and leaf through a few, you can learn more about the library's prestigious list of awards. It was Canada's first LEED-certified library. It won the Lieutenant Governor of BC Award for Architecture in 2009, and also the Sustainable Architecture and Building Canadian Green Building Award in 2010. It's a library that everyone loves for all it provides for the community.

Address 4329 Main Street, Whistler, BC V8E 1B2, +1 (604) 935-8435, www.whistlerlibrary.ca, publicservices@whistlerlibrary.ca | Getting there From the Sea to Sky Highway, exit onto Village Gate Boulevard and turn left onto Northlands Boulevard, then turn right onto Main Street. | Hours Daily 10am–5pm | Tip Sitting by the fireplace is a great place to read books in the Winter, but in the summer check out the absolutely gorgeous and peaceful little pond surrounded by lawn chairs in Florence Petersen Park right behind the library.

53 Lightboard Rendezvous
A cool place to meet

It's probably one of the busiest and coldest meeting points in Canada. The short directive, "I'll meet you at the Lightboard by the Round-house," is exchanged by countless skiers every season. With 38 lifts on the resort, there's lots of room for confusion amongst its annual two million skiing visitors when it comes to meeting up. But the old and trusted wooden lightboard tower by the Roundhouse, which has been standing there since 1979 like a beacon calling out to reunite family and friends, leaves very little room for misinterpretation. It's partly because of its size – it's 9 metres (30 feet) high – and the attention it garners as it disseminates information on the status and traffic for 14 key lifts. It truly is a cool place to meet.

It begins lighting up like a Christmas tree first thing in the morning. Technicians from the Lift Maintenance Department rise early and are responsible for personally riding each chairlift from bottom to top, ensuring its safe operation. They literally "green light" each lift the go-ahead via radio to the Lift Operations Center building near the lightboard. Throughout the day, dozens of liftees, the denizens of those small shacks you see at the top of each chairlift, monitor stoppages and traffic flow. They continually relay live information to the Operations Center, where lights are switched on and off. Although the Lightboard by the Roundhouse is the most iconic, there are half a dozen other ones located in key locations throughout both mountains, all controlled from the Operations Center building.

At the end of each day, a reverse process takes place. This time working on a predetermined schedule, and with input from the ski patrol and the Mountain Manager, liftees begin shutting down each lift. Information is again relayed into operations, and green lights turn into red lights. So what's Whistler Blackcomb's busiest lift? That's easy: it's the Emerald Chair.

Address The top of Whistler Mountain, Whistler, BC V0N 1B4, www.whistlerblackcomb.com | **Getting there** Take the Creekside Gondola or the Village Gondola. The Lightboard is about 300 metres (330 yards) from the entrance to the Rendezvous. | **Hours** See website for gondola schedule | **Tip** Get your skis off, jump on a big inner tube, and enjoy the bliss of sliding on snow. The Bubly Tube Park is open till 6pm (4545 Blackcomb Way).

54 M Creek Bridge Disaster
A tragic and terrifying night

When Mother Nature collides with any man-made structure, and they fight, Mother Nature usually wins. Case in point: a small, old, wooden trestle bridge on the Sea to Sky Highway, that in the wee hours of the morning of October 28, 1981 was completely obliterated by unrelenting torrential rains. The unremarkable M Creek Bridge was the scene of the most horrific and disturbing multiple motor vehicle accident in BC history. Four cars travelling on the road that morning proceeded through the heavy rain and winds, unaware that the bridge ahead of them no longer existed – it had been completely swept away in the storm. Each car plunged over the steep embankment, resulting in eight fatalities. A ninth body was later recovered from Howe Sound, where the creek runs into the ocean, but it was determined that it had gone off one of several other bridges that were destroyed on the road that night.

Joe Chisholm, one driver who miraculously lived to tell the tale, was driving his car across the M Creek Bridge at 12:30am when the wall of mud hit. According to the UPI archives, he said, "The bridge just crumbled, you couldn't go left, you couldn't go right. It was pitch black, I put the brakes on but there was nothing for them to hold onto. The car was out in the air." Another driver, who stopped in the nick of time just before the missing bridge, witnessed two cars plunge into the creek. In the darkness and confusion, he warned other cars to stop. The aftermath of the disaster resulted in thousands of tourists being stranded in Whistler until the highway was finally reopened. At the time Whistler's Achilles' heel was that only one road led in and out of the resort municipality. The Duffy Lake Road was opened in 1992 as a secondary, albeit much longer way to make it back to Vancouver.

You can easily observe the new fortified M Creek Bridge as you drive over its solid concrete footing.

Address M Creek Bridge, Sea to Sky Highway, Whistler, BC V0N 2E0 | Getting there From the Sea to Sky Highway, drive towards Horseshoe Bay. The bridge is about 10 kilometres (6.2 miles) north of the Horseshoe Bay. | Hours Unrestricted | Tip Take a break from the road and stop at Lions Bay General Store and Café, just 2.5 kilometres (1.6 miles) south of M Creek Bridge (350 Centre Road).

55 Millar's Cabin Site
The Texas trapper of the Pemberton Trail

So much of Whistler's development can be traced back to a mysterious character by the name of John Millar and the cabin he once had in this area now known as Function Junction. As the story goes, Millar moved to these parts from Texas in the early 1900s after a run-in with the law. Legend has it that he may have shot someone and been on the lam. What we do know is that he had a cabin here, a stopping house, at what was then the junction of the Pemberton Trail. He supported himself by trapping and by providing overnight lodging for prospectors and adventurers. He hunted here and fished along the nearby Cheakamus River, and he was known to cut a roguish backwoods figure in his battered Stetson, buckskin coat, and broken nose.

Millar's story is remarkable not just because he was one of the first settlers in the area and because of his role in establishing what would one day become one of the most famous ski destinations in the world.

In 1911, Millar went to Vancouver to pick up supplies and to sell his beaver, muskrat, and other pelts to The Hudson Bay Company. The three-day journey involved taking a packhorse down the Pemberton Trail to Squamish, and then a steamboat the rest of the way. It was a fateful trip, for it was on this trip that he met Alex and Myrtle Philip (see ch. 39). The American couple were so enthralled by the colourful character that they made the journey to visit Millar at his cabin and enjoy his bear stew.

Sadly, the cabin, like Millar himself, is long gone. Perhaps future historians will find the precise location and place a marker on the spot. But in the meantime, when next you're in Function Junction and see this sign for Millar Creek Road, remember the rough rider who settled here and who's wild tales of the outdoors lured others away from the big city, and who, in his small and unknowing way, lit the spark that would become Whistler.

Address Millar's cabin was located in the area now known as Function Junction, about 4 kilometres (2.5 miles) south of Whistler's Creekside Village on the Sea to Sky Highway. | **Getting there** From the Sea to Sky Highway, take the Alpha Lake Road exit, and there you are. | **Hours** Unrestricted | **Tip** Modern-day adventure seekers should check out the made-in-Whistler skis and snowboards from Prior (1410 Alpha Lake Road, No. 104, www.priorsnow.com).

56__The Missing Airmen

Mystery of flight 21454

On March 22, 1956, Royal Canadian Airforce flight officers Gerald Stubbs and James Miller were flying their Canadair T-33 Silver Star jet on a routine training flight out of the 409 Squadron's base near Comox on Vancouver Island. The jet could reach a top speed of just under 1000 kph (620 mph) and had a range of 2,000 kilometres (1,250 miles). They were expected to be gone for about an hour. But just 17 minutes into the flight, radar showed them facing poor weather. And they were never seen again.

What happened to them remained a mystery for years. No one suspected they bailed out over the Callaghan Valley, 140 kilometres (87 miles) west of the base until local mountaineer Howard Rode stumbled across a piece of the aircraft's canopy high up on Mount Callaghan in 1974. He noted the serial number, and the first piece of the puzzle came together. Two decades later, in 1998, the full wreck was found 4 kilometres (2.5 miles) south of the canopy's location when an airborne firefighter from the BC Forest Service spotted it from above. An investigation showed the plane's Rolls-Royce engines had been starved of fuel.

Then later, in 2010, another intriguing clue surfaced: the remains of a helmet identified as belonging to Stubbs or Miller by its squadron colors was found between the wreck and the canopy. Could it be they bailed out, survived the crash, and lived among the snow, forest, and bears? Are their ejected seats still resting somewhere between the wreck and the canopy? Time may tell.

There are two memorials to the missing airmen. The most accessible one is this one located here at the Alexander Falls viewing platform. Howard Rode placed another of his own making near where he found the canopy. The retrieved helmet is preserved at the Whistler Museum (see ch. 38).

Address Alexander Falls, Squamish-Lillooet, BC V0N 1B1, www.vancouvertrails.com/blog/alexander-falls | **Getting there** From the Sea to Sky Highway, exit onto Callaghan Valley Road. Follow signs toward Whistler Olympic Park and look for the Alexander Falls sign. | **Hours** Unrestricted | **Tip** Experience the breathtaking sites of Whistler from above on a flight with Blackcomb Helicopters (9960 Heliport Road, www.blackcombhelicopters.com).

57__Moe Joe's Nightclub
Trudeau bounced here

For almost two years at the end of the last century, the Rogue Wolf Nightclub stood at this location and served the boisterous youth who skied by day and partied by night. In that regard, it was not so different from many bars that cater to a mountain-crawling clientele. But for a few months in 1997, this was the place where Canada's glamorous 23rd prime minister, Justin Trudeau, worked as a doorman and bouncer in between shifts as a snowboard instructor with Whistler-Blackcomb's "Ride Tribe" ski school.

Those were the days when the Resort Municipality of Whistler had so many liquor licenses that it was the most heavily licensed jurisdiction, per capita, in all of BC. Despite all those licenses, or perhaps because of them, competition in the bar business was tough – too tough for the Rogue Wolf. Plagued with financial and other difficulties, and with their charming bouncer having moved back to Vancouver to study at UBC, the Rogue was shut down and had its assets seized by the province in 1998.

But where there is risk there is also opportunity. So for veteran club owner Joel Springman, former manager of Garfinkel's Pub, the Rogue's demise was good news. He bought it, renovated it, and re-invented it as Moe Joe's Nightclub.

Today, Moe Joe's is "Whistler's No. 1 Nightclub" and one of the best places to party the night away. Come on Sunday night for the Glow Party (glow sticks and face paint provided at the door), and come back again for "Recovery Mondays," when happy hour prices keep the party going until 11pm.

The Trudeau connection to Whistler's good times goes back to 1971, when then 51-year-old Prime Minister Pierre Trudeau ended his bachelor days by honeymooning here with his 22-year-old hippie bride Margaret Sinclair.

Address 4115 Golfers Approach, Whistler, BC V8E 0M2, +1 (604) 935-1152, www.moejoes.com | Getting there From the Sea to Sky Highway, exit onto Village Gate Boulevard and take your first right onto Gateway Drive. Park at the public parking, then walk south on Rainbow Plaza and turn left at Golfer's Approach. | Hours Thu–Mon 9pm–2am | Tip Who knows where Justin Trudeau gets his snowboards, but you might try buying or renting yours at Showcase Snowboards (4340 Sundial Crescent).

58 Mountain WoMan Fish & Chips

Queen of the road

Some of the world's best fish and chips shops are found in the most unusual places, and this is one of them. Located on the east side of Highway 99 as you enter the old mining town of Britannia Beach, this spot built around an old school bus has been serving hearty grub to travellers since 1984. It was started by a couple who originally named the business Mountain Man, but when the man left, the owner Lynne Cook cleverly tacked a "Wo" sign onto it and carried on solo. So now it's Mountain WoMan Fish & Chips.

This spot is a landmark as famous as Vancouver's steam clock, and the patrons are so steadfast and loyal, some second generation – people who used to eat here with their parents and are now taking their own kids. Of course it's also had a lot of visits from people just passing through. Seven-foot-tall NBA superstar Kareem Abdul-Jabbar had to crouch down to get in. Leslie Nielsen, star of *Airplane* and *Naked Gun* didn't have that problem. *Home Improvement* star Tim Allen resisted the urge to try and start the bus. More recently Freddie Highmore, star of TV's *The Good Doctor*, stopped in for a bite.

In addition to fish and chips, you can also get a good burger here – hamburger, fish burger, buffalo burger, chicken burger, or veggie burger. Or just enjoy a milkshake as you watch the parade of vehicles up and down the Sea to Sky Highway.

The blue schoolbus at the heart of this establishment is a classic 1975 model made by the Thomas Built Buses Company, headquartered in North Carolina. Founded in 1916, the company is the oldest surviving bus manufacturer in North America, and it was family-run until the early 2000s. This particular school bus served kids in North Vancouver and was affectionately called "Thumper."

Address Copper Beach Estates, Highway 99, Britannia Beach, BC V0N 1J0, +1 (604) 896-2468 | Getting there From the Sea to Sky Highway, exit onto Copper Drive and take the first left. | Hours Mon–Thu 9:30am–4:30pm, Fri 11am–6pm, Sat & Sun 11:45am–5:30pm | Tip Lynne's son Ryan is a big deal in the chainsaw wood-carving community. You can see one of his works outside the Britannia Beach firehall, just down Copper Drive.

59__The Mushroom House

The most famous house in Whistler

Over a period of 25 years, eccentric Whistler artist Zube Aylward built what came to be known as "The Mushroom House." Was it named for the psychedelic properties of a certain type of forest fungi, or was it simply its organic natural shape and form that gave it that peculiar moniker? Who's to say for sure, although Aylward's creativity was undoubtedly influenced by his organic surroundings. Completed in 2002, the 372-square-metre (4,200-square-foot) home has an exterior inspired by the glacial formations around its location and an interior themed around the anatomy of a tree, with roots at the bottom, ground on the middle, and plenty of branches on the upper level. There's hardly a right angle in the entire building. You'd not be the first one to think it was designed by Dr. Seuss for the residents of Whoville.

It is said Aylward would often accumulate pieces for the house from the forests nearby and use them for various things, like the spiraling wooden staircase with spiderweb banisters and the stonework around the fireplace. Elsewhere there is impressive ceramic tilework on the floor and stained glass in the windows, and it even has its own grotto – probably the most unique après ski destination in all of Whistler. It's a remarkable structure.

Aylward built the house as a home for himself and his wife Pat, yet in the end it has turned out to be his signature work of art. Everything is original and handmade. Margaret Trudeau, Heidi Klum, The Tragically Hip, The Dave Matthews Band, and others count among the house's past guests and admirers.

The Mushroom is a private home, and so legend has it that when the time came to sell the house in 2007 to new owners, Aylward took inspiration from the cryptogram on Gaudi's famous Sagrada Familia Cathedral, which has 16 numbers that can be added together in hundreds of different combinations but always add up to 33.

Address 9464 Emerald Drive, Whistler, BC V0N | Getting there From the Sea to Sky Highway, exit onto Emerald Drive, turn right onto Pinetree Lane, then continue straight back onto Emerald Drive. | Hours Unrestricted from the outside only | Tip A great place for a picnic lunch is nearby Emerald Park (Sea to Sky Highway and Emerald Drive, www.whistler.ca/culture-recreation/parks/neighborhood-parks).

60_North Arm Farm

Family, food, and farm-life fantasy

North Arm Farm is a great place for the whole family. It has chickens, pigs, sheep, an old tractor, a swing set made from two giant telephone poles, and a stunning mountain view. You'll also find some of the best locally grown produce and homemade jam and ice cream.

Here you can find three types of cauliflower, five different varieties of potato, six different kinds of radish, eleven varieties of squash, all the kales, burdock, salsify, sunchoke, and a host of all the usual suspects like beets, cabbage, garlic, peas, strawberries, raspberries, blackberries, and more. The produce is so plentiful, so good, and so unique, that restaurants in Whistler – and some in Vancouver – choose to source from here for their menus.

Resident chef Brock Windsor combines farm ingredients to make hearty and satisfying food for you to enjoy here or take home. The farm's shop also has some amazing pickled items, like pickled garlic scapes, and a terrific strawberry-rhubarb jam. And don't pass up their farm life-inspired ice cream: blueberry, raspberry, and other limited editions created according to the whims of nature's bounty. If you like, you can also pick your own, where they charge by the pound.

Owners Trish and Jordan Sturdy bought this 22-hectare (54-acre) corn farm in 1993 and have spent decades converting it into a place where their family, and yours, can come together over good food. Initially, there was just one old barn with a dirt floor, but over the years, the farm itself and its reputation have grown. People loved the farm as much as the produce.

There are now places to sit and enjoy a snack or even to host an event, as the stunning mountain view and rustic setting are the backdrop for epic wedding pictures. Kids are free to roam around the open spaces and try out that amazing swing, play on the old tractor, hide out in the old pig shed, or meet the livestock.

Address 1888 Sea to Sky Highway, Pemberton, BC V0N 2L0, +1 (604) 894-5379, www.northarmfarm.com | Getting there From Whistler, head north on the Sea to Sky Highway for about 5 kilometres (3 miles) past the main turnoff for Pemberton and watch for the signs on your right. | Hours Daily 9am–6pm | Tip Visit the Pemberton Farmers' Market at the downtown Community Barn on Fridays from 3–6pm June through October (7444 Frontier Street, www.pemberton farmers market.com).

61 — The Old Steam Donkey

A hike to hidden history

There are plenty of stunning hikes and trails throughout the entire Sea to Sky area, but if you like a hike with a little history on the side, the DeBeck's Hill Trail at Alice Lake Provincial Park is the one for you. The hike isn't terribly long (3 kilometres/1.88 miles round trip), and the trail isn't a challenging one. But it does have a good incline (275 metres/900 feet in elevation), so if you go at a pace, your muscles will burn, and you'll surely break a sweat. A little past the halfway mark, the trees give way to open rock face that's popular with climbers. Press on a bit further, and you'll discover the wreck of a mysterious machine called a "steam donkey."

If you're an alert hiker, you will have noticed various bits of old steel cable along the route. These, like the steam donkey, are evidence of the hill's past role in BC's lumber industry. Dennis DeBeck had a sawmill around here from 1946–1966, after almost 20 years logging in the Parkhurst area of Whistler (see ch. 68). Like a lot of people in those days, he used a steam donkey, which is a steam-powered power plant with gears that turned one or more drums or winches to lift, drag, and move logs from the stump to an accumulation point. The donkeys were often mobile units. While this one hasn't been moved in over 50 years, it's still mounted on wooden skids.

Logging was a huge business in these parts, and steam donkeys like this one quickly replaced horses and oxen as the source of industrial power. The game-changing machine was invented in California in 1881 and had a huge impact on British Columbia. By the late 1920s, almost one out of every ten people in the province was employed in the logging industry. By 1930, the total value of production in BC was nearly $100M. You can see other examples of early industrial power in other places, but it's rare to find one abandoned in the same place it was last used.

Address Alice Lake Provincial Park, Squamish, BC V0N 1H0, +1 (604) 986-9371, www.env.gov.bc.ca/bcparks/explore/parkpgs/alice_lk | Getting there Exit the Sea to Sky Highway at Alice Lake Road, about 40 kilometres (25 miles) south of Whistler. Go past the first parking lot and the Information Centre to the second parking lot. Follow DeBeck's Hill Trail. | Hours See website for schedule | Tip If the donkey has renewed your love of local lumber, why not take some home in the form of custom wood furniture handcrafted by Warren & Wayne (39012 Discovery Way, www.warrenandwayne.com).

62 Oldest Building in Town
A tale in three parts at Whistler Municipal Hall

There are three very unusual things you might be surprised to learn about Whistler's oldest building. First of all, it only dates back to the mid-1970s. Second, though it is now a serious place, it used to be one of the hottest night spots in town. And third – maybe strangest of all – it was originally located somewhere else, cut into several pieces, and moved to its present location on the back of a truck!

This building actually started life as a Keg N Cleaver Restaurant built on Crabapple Drive near the Adventures West Village, a condo development on the north end of Alta Lake. That Keg, designed by William Dunn and Associates, opened its doors in 1974 and soon became one of the most popular social centres in Whistler at that time, a place of only about 1,000 permanent residents. The building included a cafeteria where condo dwellers and weekend revelers could dine at any time of day. The dinner menu included prime rib, sirloin, New York strip steaks, salmon, and lobster, all within a price range of $5.25 to $6.75. But that's not all. The restaurant also doubled as a nightclub and had a dance floor with a DJ booth up in the rafters. Legend also has it that Canadian rock band Doug and The Slugs performed many of their earliest pre-fame gigs here in the 1970s.

When it became clear that the focal point of Whistler was going to be elsewhere, the Keg's owners left the Alta Lake building to start a new restaurant at Whistler Village Inn. The original building was left vacant. But since the newly formed Resort Municipality of Whistler needed a municipal hall, it seemed to make more sense to cut the Keg into three sections and have it moved to its present location on Blackcomb Way than to build a new building. The building was moved here on the back of a truck in 1981. So next time you're in Whistler Municipal Hall, don't be surprised if you have a sudden craving for a juicy sirloin steak.

Address Whistler Municipal Hall, 4325 Blackcomb Way, Whistler, BC V0N 1B4, +1 (604) 932-5535, www.whistler.ca | **Getting there** From the Sea to Sky Highway, exit at Village Gate and turn left on Blackcomb Way. Park at first right. | **Hours** Mon–Fri 8am–4:30pm | **Tip** There's still a Keg at Whistler Village Inn, but these days you'll have to pay more than five dollars for a steak (4429 Sundial Place, www.kegsteakhouse.com).

63 Olympic Medal Haul
Go for Olympic gold, silver, and bronze at City Hall

Unless you've actually won an Olympic Winter Games medal, which is very rare, or you know someone who has, they are not that easy to view. After all, only a finite number of them are minted every four years, and most of those are taken home by top competitors. For the 2010 Olympic Winter Games, a total 615 medals were struck by the Royal Canadian Mint. Each gold, silver and bronze medal is a piece of artwork in its own right, and a modest little collection of all three medals sits in the public lobby of Whistler's small City Hall. Not far from the hall's front entrance door, next to the counter where you pay your taxes and parking tickets, you'll find a well-lit display case housing these historical mementos.

The medals feature original aboriginal West Coast designs depicting an Orca and a Raven. They were part of a collaborative effort between two Vancouver-based artists. Omer Arbel and Corrine Hunt's design submission was selected over 47 other entries from across Canada and around the world. After the winning design was finally chosen, the Mint in Ottawa managed a 30-step process to produce each one carefully. That process required the skilled craftsmanship of 34 engineers, engravers, die technicians, and machinists.

The result was an Olympic Games "first" in that each medal is totally unique. They are struck from different parts of one big original piece of art. By way of explanation, every medal includes its own unique and signature element of the larger orca and raven artwork, such as the trace of the orca's eye, the curve of its dorsal fin, or the contours of the raven's wing. Local Olympic Organizing Committees love "firsts," and these medals are not flat like the kind handed out at every other Olympics. No, instead they have an undulating surface which represents the West Coast landscape of mountains, waves, and three-dimensional drifting snow.

Address 4325 Blackcomb Way, Whistler, BC V8E 0X5, +1 (604) 932-5535, www.whistler.ca | Getting there From the Sea to Sky Highway, take the Village Gate exit, turn left on Blackcomb Way, and then park at first right. | Hours Daily 8am–4:30pm | Tip Not far from City Hall is Fire Hall Number One. Walk over from the Municipal Hall to see an old-fashioned fireman's pole – the silver shiny kind they slide down. It's visible through the large outside windows, but you can't slide down it unless you become a firefighter yourself (4315 Village Gate Boulevard).

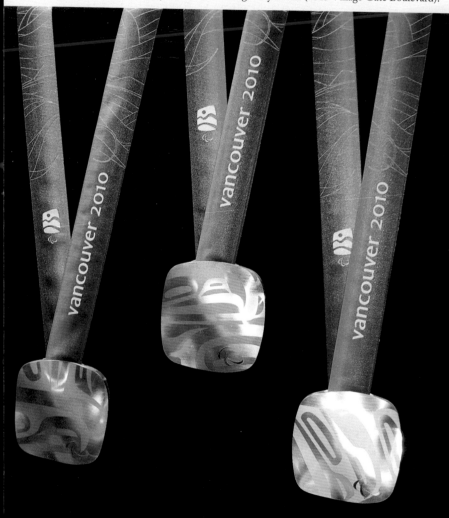

64 Olympic Plaza Ice Rink
A famous and loved Canadian winter pastime

Few things are more quintessentially Canadian than practicing hockey on a flooded lawn that's been frozen over and converted into an ice rink. In the winter, the Municipality of Whistler does just that at the Olympic Plaza stage. It's a super cool (literally) experience to skate in the heart of the Whistler Village with amazing views of the nearby mountains behind you, the iconic Olympic rings above you, and thousands of festive lights twinkling around you.

Skating here is divided into three sections, and it's all family friendly. One section is covered, which comes in handy with all the snow Whistler gets. Another section is cordoned off for hockey and figure skating. And the third section is the large, free-for-all, flooded lawn. Skating is free. And you can bring your own skates or rent a pair for $5. If you are an absolute beginner, you'll be taken care of too with helmets supplied at no charge. The rink will also provide, also free of charge, a "skate aid," which looks and functions like a walker on ice – you can hold on to it for balance. For the perfect ending to your ultimate outdoor, frozen-lawn skating experience, treat yourself to a cup of steaming and delicious hot chocolate from one of the many cafés and restaurants near the rink.

Once you've built up your confidence and honed your skills, you may want to consider venturing out for another amazing Canadian experience: skating on one of the many frozen lakes at Whistler. When conditions are right, skating is possible on the local lakes. But, and this is a BIG but, it can be very dangerous and should only be done when the weather has created a safe and very thick sheet of ice.

Finally, if lawns or lakes don't tickle your fancy, Whistler also has its very own indoor, NHL-sized ice surface at the Meadow Park Sports Centre just up the road on HWY 99. The ice there never melts, and it is impossible to fall through it.

Address 4365 Blackcomb Way, Whistler, BC V0N 1B4, +1 (604) 935-7529 and press 3, www.whistler.ca/culture-recreation/facilities/outdoor-skating-rink, recreation@whistler.ca | Getting there From the Sea to Sky Highway, exit onto Lorimer Road, turn right onto Blackcomb Way. Parking on the left. | Hours See website for schedule | Tip The 2010 Olympic Torch Relay involved 12,000 individuals carrying the flame from coast to coast over a 106-day period. A large white symbolic torch statue sits opposite the ice rink in the Olympic Plaza to commemorate the journey.

65 The Olympic Ski Jumps
No women allowed

Huge ski jumps, the kind you see every four years at the Winter Olympics, are uncommon and expensive structures. The sport used to get good television ratings but ranks low in general participation. Think about it: how many parents do you know who encourage their kids to take up ski jumping? Besides, there are very few big ski jump training facilities left in Canada. There was one in Calgary built for the 1988 Olympic Winter Games, but it has shut down, and there was one in Thunder Bay, that has closed too. But the one built in 2007 for the 2010 Olympic Winter Games is still operational.

Because these jumps are so majestic and massive to behold, and because they are becoming so rare, it's worth the trip up to the Callaghan Valley to see the 95-metre and the 125-metre jumps, even with no events or snow. If you're fortunate enough to time your visit with a competition, though, nothing beats watching the athletes, skis attached, rocketing through the air after launching themselves off one of those long ramps at speeds of up to 95 kph (60 mph).

It's an amazing sport to watch, but during the 2010 Olympic Winter Games, ski jumping got worldwide attention for all the wrong reasons. Leading up to the Games, the IOC outraged ski jumpers worldwide by excluding women. They declared the women's sport not developed enough for inclusion in the Olympic Games, while claiming men's ski-jumping was an acceptable event. In 2008, a group of women athletes sued the IOC for gender discrimination. The IOC's position was there must be at least two world championships held in a sport for it to be considered sufficiently developed to be part of the Winter Olympic Games. So there were no women launched off those ramps at the 2010 Games. However, the IOC reversed their decision and let women participate in the 2014 Winter Games held in Russia.

Address 5 Callaghan Valley Road, Whistler, BC V0N 1B0, +1 (604) 964-0059, www.whistlersportlegacies.com | Getting there From the Sea to Sky Highway, exit at Callaghan Valley Road and drive 10 kilometres (6.2 miles) to the ski jump. | Hours See website for seasonal hours | Tip Located on the upper level of the Day Lodge is a café open daily throughout the season for a hearty meal or a warm drink. They can accommodate most dietary needs too (5 Callaghan Valley Road, www.whistlersportlegacies.com/ whistler-olympic-park/day-lodge).

66 — Original Rainbow Lodge
Where it all started

Long before the Resort Municipality of Whistler came into existence, there was a little place on Alta Lake called Rainbow Lodge. It burned down in 1977, but you can still visit the three original guest cabins located at the entrance to Rainbow Park – the last remnants of a romantic past and stoic reminder of the historic lodge that first enticed visitors to what would become one of the world's most famous resort destinations.

The story of the Lodge goes back over 100 years when a young American couple named Alex and Myrtle Philip purchased 10 acres of land on the west side of Alta Lake from local trapper Charlie Chandler (see ch. 39). They had moved to British Columbia in their twenties, newly wed and full of dreams of a new life in the remote and ruggedly beautiful Canadian West.

With savings of $700, they bought the land from Chandler in 1913. By 1914 – the same year the railway line came to Alta Lake – the Lodge was open for business. The pristine and remote destination quickly thrived. By the 1930s, the Philips had added 45 outbuildings, including a general store, a horse-stable, tennis courts, post office, and a dedicated railway station. Rainbow Lodge advertisements boasted that it was the most popular tourist resort west of Jasper.

The Philips' ran the Lodge for 30 years, selling it to Alec and Audrey Greenwood in 1948 for the princely sum of $100,000. The Greenwoods ran the Lodge until 1970. By then, Whistler was already entering a new phase as a destination for winter sport enthusiasts and a potential location for the Winter Olympic Games.

It's a shame Rainbow Lodge no longer exists. But, as you stand here by the old cabins, gaze out over the lake and say a word of thanks for Alex and Myrtle who also once stood on this very spot and saw a place so beautiful that it had to be shared with the world.

Address 5778 Alta Lake Road, Whistler, BC V0N 0A0, www.artswhistler.com/location/rainbow-park-cabins | **Getting there** From the Sea to Sky Highway, exit onto Alta Lake Road exit and follow its winding way to destination. | **Hours** Unrestricted | **Tip** Food trucks visit daily from June to September. Check out their schedules on the Whistler website (www.whistler.ca/culture-recreation/parks/food-trucks/food-truck-schedule).

67__Our Lady of the Mountains Church

An important place to worship

Canada's first ecumenical chapel was built in 1968 right at the base of Whistler Mountain. The simple A-frame building only held 60 people. Skiers would often come in on Sunday mornings with their skis and poles, ready for mass but secretly hoping it wouldn't last for too long so that they could hit the slopes. Eventually, as the mountain's popularity grew, it attracted more skiers from around the world, many of them Catholics, looking for a welcoming place to worship.

At the same time, Whistler's vibrant local Catholic population expanded organically. As many as 800 churchgoers, from different faiths would show up for services each year. The A-frame quickly became woefully inadequate, and the faithful began using other shared spaces, like the local elementary school and the old local conference center. The community needed a new, larger church.

In 1994, construction began on a new building in a new location alongside a strand of trees. Since it was an important dream of the Whistler Catholic community to have a larger house of worship, it was appropriate that the new 3,000-square-foot church be built next to the River of Golden Dreams. The church, which is accented by cedar logs, blends into the overall Whistler architecture. The austere wooden cross that sits in front of the Church, with a beautiful mountain backdrop, is a reminder of the Parish's humble beginnings.

Since its completion, the church has become a place to gather and worship, to rest, to learn, and to meet new friends. Many locals, even those who don't attend services there, have visited the new building. By moving a temporary wall before the wooden altar and rearranging the chairs, the church quickly transforms into a beautiful banquet hall or versatile event space.

Address 6299 Lorimer Road, Whistler, BC V6E 0C5, +1 (604) 905-4781, www.whistlercatholicchurch.ca, whistlercatholicchurch@telus.net | Getting there From the Sea to Sky Highway, exit at Lorimer Road. | Hours Unrestricted from outside; see website for services schedule | Tip Not far from the Church a bit further down the trail is an interesting fish ladder on a tributary of the River of Golden Dreams. If you head south on the Valley Trail about 350 metres (380 yards) and look to your right, you will spot it.

68 Parkhurst Ghost Town
Whistler's twilight zone

To see the ghosts, you must first know their history. It goes like this: back in 1926, widow Parkhurst sold this patch of land to the Barr Brothers. Ross, William, and Malcolm Barr were loggers by trade and thought this an ideal site to start a mill. So they built and ran their lumber company here until selling it in 1932 to two men named B.C. Keeley and Byron Smith. Keeley and Smith rebranded the business Northern Mills the next year.

Ross Barr stayed on to manage the mill, along with another man, Denis DeBeck (see ch. 61). The mill was a successful enterprise, at one time employing and accommodating up to 70 loggers. And there was even a small school house and a store to accommodate the loggers and their families. But it also had its darker days. The Great Depression pretty much wiped the business out financially, and a spectacular fire reduced the mill to ashes in 1938.

The mill rose again after the fire, but business eventually petered out in the late 1950s. By the late 1960s and early 1970s, no one was left here except transient hippies, beatniks, and American draft dodgers preferring the fir, hemlock, cedar, and spruce trees of BC to the palm and bamboo trees of Vietnam.

All that remains here now looks like a set from *The Twilight Zone*. A hike up to the ghost town rewards the curious with echoes of the past and faded remnants of another era. You may see some old cars and some rusted appliances and artefacts scattered about. One of the abandoned buildings has been used as a canvas by present-day graffiti artists for their creative pursuits (some with more success than others). If you are a photographer or an Instagrammer, the site will offer up some interesting images contrasting the decaying past with pop art. It's a feast for the eyes and the imagination. Rumour has it that nearby Green Lake has a monster on its shores – a giant abandoned tractor.

Address Parkhurst Ghost Town is on the east side of Green Lake, www.hikingforthescaredycat.com/parkhurst-ghost-town-whistler.html | **Getting there** From Whistler Village, drive 11 kilometres (6.8 miles) north on the Sea to Sky Highway, pass Green Lake, and exit right at Gravel Pit Road. Cross the tracks and the bridge, and follow the dirt road to the right. After 2 kilometres (1.25 miles), the road ends at a concrete barrier. The path to the Ghost Town begins here. | **Hours** Unrestricted | **Tip** If the ghost town has given you a taste for remote trails and off-road terrain, take your curiosity to the next level with Whistler ATV (2 Callaghan Road, www.whistleratv.com).

69__The Pangea Pod Hotel
Small but posh

If you are looking for a spacious hotel room at Whistler with a king-sized bed, a big desk, fridge, minibar, and large screen TV, then save yourself some time and skip this chapter. But before you do though, think about this: when you go to Whistler, it's mainly for the wide-open spaces of the great outdoors. Is the size of your hotel room really all that important? After all, most of the time, you're just sleeping in it. With that philosophy in mind, owners Jelena and Russell Kling launched their 88-pod, capsule-sized accommodation hotel the Pangea in the summer of 2018. Before that, the couple spent years travelling around the world staying at hostels, homes, and hotels, and everything in between, which informed the design and development of their very own prototype capsule hotel.

As for the pods themselves, they have all you'll ever need when you're tired and longing to bunk down after a long day exploring Whistler. Each pod is designed to accommodate one or two people and has the first thing everyone looks for in a room nowadays – a USB charging point. The pods also have privacy curtains, mirrors, a fan, hangers, cool artwork, soft LED lighting, a shelving unit, a lockable cabinet, and luggage storage. The comfy mattress has fresh, clean sheets. Don't worry about storing your gear, as the Pangea has a secured room called the Toybox, meant for skis and boards. There is a nice bar called the Living Room that serves a variety of craft beers and good quality wines, and the small rooftop patio bar is a great place to chill and meet other guests.

This spot does not feel like a budget hotel. Pod and capsule hotels are becoming more and more popular among young, budget-conscious travelers in places like Amsterdam, Tokyo, and Singapore. The Pangea Whistler is the first hotel of its kind in Canada, and the name is based on a throwback to when the world was one big continent.

Address 4333 Sunrise Alley, Whistler, BC V8E 1M7, +1 (604) 962-1011, www.pangeapod.com | **Getting there** From the Sea to Sky Highway, exit onto Village Gate Boulevard and then turn right onto Blackcomb Way, and right again onto Sundial Crescent, to Sunrise Valley. | **Hours** Call for hours | **Tip** After saving some money by staying in a pod hotel, why not splurge on an amazing dinner at Araxia? It is one of the best restaurants in the Village and just a few steps away (4222 Village Square, No. 110, www.araxi.com).

70 Peak 2 Peak Gondola

Breaking two world records

There are certain structures you see that leave a pit in your stomach and your jaw wide open as you wonder, "How the hell did they do that?" Peak 2 Peak Gondola is one of them.

It's not exactly one of the Eight Wonders of the Modern World, but it comes close. Up until 2017, the gondola held the record for the longest free span between conveyor ropeway towers, at 3.03 kilometres (1.8 miles) to be exact. When it opened in 2008, this engineering marvel captured the world's attention and was the subject of a documentary on the Discovery Channel called *Peak 2 Peak: Building the World's Biggest Gondola*. And the History Channel featured it on the popular program, *Modern Marvels*.

To give you an idea of the project's magnitude, let's start by considering just the cable that transports the 28 sky cabins, each holding 28 people. It was made in Switzerland and shipped over in five separate spools. The only problem was that since each spool weighed over 90 tons, there was only one harbour crane on the West Coast of North America capable of handling such an incredibly heavy load. That crane was in Vancouver. Except the crane was in the Port of Vancouver, *Washington*. The spools were then loaded onto a train to Whistler, where a crew of 80 workers spent an entire summer installing the cable.

Although the Zugspitze Mountain in Germany snatched away the tower span world record from the Peak 2 Peak Gondola in 2017, Whistler can lay claim to another important world gondola record. The Peak 2 Peak Gondola terminal buildings, one at the Whistler Roundhouse Lodge and one at Blackcomb Mountain's Rendezvous Lodge, are the two largest lift terminals in the world.

The entire project took almost 10 years to complete and came in at a cost of $50 million. The payoff today is that 4,100 people per hour can now travel between the two mountains in about 11 minutes.

Address The top of Whistler Mountain, Whistler, BC V0N 1B4, www.whistlerblackcomb.com | **Getting there** Take the Creekside Gondola or the Village Gondola. | **Hours** See website for gondola hours | **Tip** The terminus of the Peak to Peak Gondola on the Whistler side is the modern Doug Forseth building. Doug is an active, knowledgeable, and well known Whistler resident who worked in senior executive positions on the Mountain for over 23 years. Take a few moments to admire the building's sleek lines and cool architecture.

71 The Peak to Creek Run
North America's longest consistent ski run

Since its inception, Whistler has used different advertising slogans. No moniker was more appropriate than "The Long Run Mountain," which was promoted in various marketing campaigns throughout North America. The campaign was a refreshing example of truth in advertising: the world-famous Peak to Creek Run is 11 kilometres (7 miles) long. For those of you who believe that that may have been a typo, let's repeat the salient point: *seven miles long*.

Seven miles of amazing scenery offers lots of bumps and turns and different grades and steep pitches along the way. It takes the average person about 25 minutes of non-stop skiing just to make it down. It's worth the effort, and you will be rewarded with burning thighs, tired lungs, and an incredible cardio workout – and memories that will last for years to come. And the minute you make it down, after resting, here's one word of advice: repeat. If the Peak to Creek run doesn't have enough vertical fall for you, then try Franz's run. It has the greatest vertical fall of any ski run in North America.

Whistler and Blackcomb have numerous Black Double Diamond runs with lots of challenging terrain for advanced and expert skiers. Most people will never be able to master these steep and deep dangerous downhill routes, so it is fun just to know their names and to dream. The best name goes to Spanky's Ladder, where you can expect some very tight turns and the opportunity for lots of airtime. The aptly named Coffin is a narrow corridor that can be viewed from the Peak Chair. And finally, an article in *Condé Nast Traveler* included the Couloir Extreme in their list of "Most Terrifying Ski Slopes in the World."

If all of these daredevil descriptions are having you considering a refund on your lift tickets, don't worry. Whistler and Blackcomb have an abundance of bunny runs and beginner and intermediate trails for every level of skiing.

Address The top of Whistler Mountain, Whistler, BC V0N 1B4, www.whistlerblackcomb.com |
Getting there Take the Creekside Gondola or the Village Gondola. From the Roundhouse,
transfer to the Peak chair. | **Hours** See website for seasonal hours | **Tip** If you take a spill
and bang yourself on the mountain, Whistler has plenty of good physiotherapy clinics.
A good one is Peak Performance Physio and Massage (4154 Village Green, No. 11,
www.peakperformancephysio.com).

72 Peak Podium
Fab photo opportunity

At the top of Whistler Mountain, just as you get off the gondola to the Roundhouse Lodge, there's a photo opportunity for you and three of your best friends atop the three-level podium. You and two of your friends can stand on it while your non-medal-placing fourth friend takes the picture. Who gets gold, silver, or bronze status on the podium and for which event are things you'll have to work out among yourselves. Maybe your achievement was skiing, maybe it was last night's trivia contest, maybe it's something best kept to yourself. Sure, it's hokey, but this will be the best photo from your trip. Behind you is a set of huge Olympic Rings and a view that goes for eternity.

Aside from being the quintessentially iconic place for a fun Whistler photo, the real podiums created for the 2010 Olympic and Paralympic Games were award-winning in their own way too. You might think the Games organizers just order podiums in bulk from Podiums R Us, but you'd be wrong. In truth, the 2010 Games had 23 handmade podiums, each made from over 200 pieces of precision-cut British Columbia wood. They featured a wavy, fluid, modern design that complimented the peaks and ridges of the coastal mountains that you see unfolding before (and behind) you.

The world's best winter athletes stood on these podiums for a total of 86 Olympic and 64 Paralympic victory ceremonies, with tears of joy, pride, relief, and exhaustion streaming down their faces. These podiums were all built, in addition to some 8,000 other pieces, at a fabrication shop called the "Fab Shop" by participants in a 30-week carpentry and work experience program for people who had yet to enter the workforce.

So, when you scramble up on this podium to immortalize your day for the history books, do so in the knowledge that every victory is a team effort. (Floral bouquet, medals, and champagne not included.)

Address The top of Whistler Mountain, Whistler, BC V0N 1B4, www.whistlerblackcomb.com | Getting there Take the Red Chair or the Olympic Gondola to the Roundhouse Lodge. You can't miss it. | Hours See website for chairlift schedule. | Tip If wooden wonders wind you up, walk around and look for the roughly half-dozen chainsaw sculptures nearby.

73 Peaked Pies

Pinnacle of pie perfection

There are a lot of peaks around Whistler. Most of them are on top of mountains, made of granite, and not very tasty. But some are on top of meat pies, made of mashed potatoes, peas, and gravy, and are delicious. These are the ones you'll find exclusively at the popular Peaked Pies restaurant created by Kerri Jones and Alex Relf in 2013.

This place's origin story is a familiar one: adventure-loving young Australian woman comes to Whistler for a brief experience, becomes bewitched by the place, and decides to stay. Meanwhile, outdoor-loving young Canadian man from Vancouver Island comes to Whistler for a brief experience, becomes bewitched, and decides to stay. But then something extraordinary happens. Australian woman pines for a classic Aussie-style meat pie. Canadian man just happens to be pretty good in the kitchen. And the rest is history.

As soon as Jones and Relf started cranking out the meat pies, people started lining up to eat them. And once you taste one, you'll understand why. Each pie is lovingly crafted from scratch using all the best ingredients: beef from Alberta, chicken from Fraser Valley, imported grass-fed butter. There's steak and Guinness pie, pork and pineapple pie, chicken apple and brie pie, curry pie, veggie pie, and of course, there's "the hopper" – kangaroo pie!

The doughy duo have even added an assortment of sweet pies, like apple crumble and berry peaked with whipped cream. Don't forget to try some Anzac biscuits and the Lamington cake. The business has been so popular since launching in Whistler that the couple have since opened a location in Vancouver, where latte-loving urbanites can get their cappuccino Aussie-style: made with cocoa. But they haven't left Whistler. Jones and Relf still live under the peaks that captured their hearts and inspired a pastry empire that has kept the pie makers and their customers hopping ever since.

Address 4369 Main Street, No. 105, Whistler, BC V0N 1B4, +1 (604) 962-4115, www.peakedpies.com | Getting there From the Sea to Sky Highway, take the Village Gate Boulevard exit and turn left on Northlands Boulevard. Take second right onto Main Street and park. | Hours Breakfast daily 8–11am, lunch daily 11am–9pm | Tip The colourful Kris Kupskay mural of Whistler legend Myrtle Philips (see ch. 39) is a five-minute walk away at Florence Petersen Park behind the Whistler Public Library (4329 Main Street).

74 _ Pemberton Distillery
Taste the valley in every sip

When you visit the Pemberton Distillery, established in 2009 by husband and wife team Tyler and Lorien Schramm, you'll be able to see – and taste – how they use traditional hand-operated, German-made copper pot stills to convert Pemberton's unique agricultural environment into remarkable spirits impossible to reproduce anywhere else in the world (see ch. 44).

One reason their spirits are so unique is that they use the "terroir" method in the distilling process. For those not up on their distillery lingo, that means the distiller creates a product that has the personality and essence of the place where it was produced, reflecting the climate, soil, and terrain of the area. Some say it even includes the personality and character of the distiller. In this case, that would include the knowledge Tyler picked up at the International Centre for Brewing and Distilling in Edinburgh. Another reason the Schramm spirits are so unique is that this place is located in Pemberton where the soil, nurtured by ancient glacial water, produces some of the best potatoes in Canada. The result is the world's first organic potato vodka, a rare potato-based gin ("one of the best on the planet," according to one national reviewer), a potato and wild herb absinthe, schnaps, and liqueurs.

But Pemberton doesn't just produce great potatoes – it also has excellent crops of fruit and grains, which the Schramms turn into organic malt whisky and apple brandy. All the Pemberton Distillery spirits are Certified Organic and BC Certified Craft. They are produced without any artificial or chemical additives, colouring, or GMO products at any stage and are all gluten-free.

Located just a short distance past the North Arm Farm (see ch. 60), the distillery's unassuming industrial steel building includes a small, cosy tasting area perfectly designed to reward your taste buds.

Address 1954 Venture Place, Pemberton, BC V0N 2L0, +1 (604) 894-0222, www.pembertondistillery.ca, info@pembertondistillery.ca | Getting there From the Sea to Sky Highway, exit onto Industrial Way, and turn right onto Venture Place. | Hours Wed–Sun 1–5pm | Tip Just around the corner, you can fill your beer growler up at Pemberton Brewing Company (1936 Stonecutter Place, www.pembertonbrewing.ca).

75 — Pitcher of Gold

The picture that raised a thousand elbows

On his way to a gold medal ceremony, still cruising on an adrenaline high, and on live national television, Canadian Olympic skeleton athlete Jon Montgomery shocked global viewers and thrilled Canadians when he was handed a pitcher of beer from an enthusiastic fan outside Black's Pub and, without breaking stride, quaffed down several hearty gulps from the oversized, two-litre (4-pint) mug of freshness. Walking down the street, with a gold medal soon to be around his neck, a mug of golden brew firmly in his hand, eyes ablaze with fresh victory, he was feted by the boisterous crowds as a conquering hero. His status as a true Canadian icon was thus established for all time. Since then, Montgomery has gone on to successfully parlay his global Olympic fame to national celebrity fame as host of *The Amazing Race Canada*, a role he's had since the show launched in 2013.

The pitcher itself also went on to gain a level of fame. Not quite the Holy Grail, but close. Word is that after the quaffing, it ended up in the hands of a private citizen who, after hosting it privately for a number of years, managed to get it back into Montgomery's mitts. But, being the generous guy that he is, Montgomery then offered it up as a charity auction item. It's now back in private hands, but probably under glass as a treasured artefact surely as famous and significant as The Last Spike, which secured Canada's first transcontinental railroad at Craigellachie in 1885.

As for Black's Pub, it is still there and has a long history in Whistler, starting life as The Original Ristorante pizzeria in 1985. Back then, it was a one-floor-only operation. The second floor was added by owner Lawrence Black a few years later (now you know why it's called "Black's"), and then for simplicity's sake, the pizzeria and pub were combined into one locale. Today, it's called a gastro pub, a place to eat and drinkt after a day on the slopes.

Address 4340 Sundial Place, No. 7, Whistler, BC V8E 1G5, +1 (888) 823-7932, www.blackspub.com | Getting there From the Whistler Ski Lift, turn around, and you'll see the destination. | Hours See website for hours | Tip If you want to buy a nice pitcher for your own home, try visiting Whistler Kitchen Works (4350 Lorimer Road, www.whistlerkitchenworks.com).

76 Porteau Cove
Fjords, ferry detours, and a WW II minesweeper

Porteau Cove, on the way to Whistler, is a short 38 kilometres (24 miles) north of Vancouver. Pulling into the quaint provincial campsite parking lot below the snow-capped mountain peaks, ocean views, and lush forest makes you feel as if you are in an isolated part of Norway, far away from civilization. Many locals driving by are probably unaware of three interesting facts about this small piece of secluded urban paradise. Until now, that is.

First of all, Porteau Cove is located at the entrance to a fjord. But it gets better. Not just any fjord, but the most southerly fjord in North America. A fjord, of course, is a narrow inlet with steep sides. Porteau Cove fits that bill with towering peaks rising straight out of Howe Sound. BC has about 40 fjords altogether. Howe Sound is the first fjord you will encounter while travelling north. As a side note, there are 1,190 fjords in Norway, but who's counting?

Another interesting feature at Porteau Cove is an overbuilt pier. That big old dock is actually an emergency ferry terminal. In the event that the Sea to Sky Highway is blocked by a rockslide or avalanche, BC Ferries can dock one of their huge ships and transport cars south to Horseshoe Bay, or north to Darrell Bay in Squamish. Standing on that dock is a great place to look up to admire the fjord, but don't forget to look down too. The only problem is that you won't see anything because the third amazing Porteau Cove secret is a sunken ship resting some 41.5 metres (136 feet) below the surface of the water. The USS *YMS-420*, a mine sweeper commissioned by the US Navy for service in World War II rests there. She has a storied past, sold to the Canadian Navy after the war and renamed the HMCS *Cordova*, and then purchased by Harbour Ferries in 1970. They renamed her the *Nakaya*, and finally she was purposely sunk in 1992, becoming one of BC's first artificial reefs.

Address Porteau Cove, Squamish-Lillooet D, BC, www.bcparks.ca/explore/parkpgs/ porteau | Getting there From the Sea to Sky Highway, take the Porteau Cove exit. | Hours Unrestricted | Tip There is no fishing off the dock, but if you have a hankering for fish and chips, the best restaurant for that is in nearby Horseshoe Bay is Troll's (6408 Bay Street, www.trollsrestaurant.com).

77 __ Rainbow Pier's Gilded Views

Whistler's waterfront real estate

One thing that people in Whistler love to talk about is real estate. Conversations amongst locals often quickly and sadly de-escalate into a "shoulda, woulda, coulda" scenario. Reluctant investors who missed their chance to buy at the right time reflect longingly upon the bygone days of the early 1970s when you could have picked up a large lot for less than $25,000. Whistler real estate has been a real roller-coaster ride ever since then, with plenty of ups and downs. But mainly ups.

Today, it is tough to find a decent-sized house in Whistler for less than $1 million. There's a strip of prime real estate on Alta Lake that recently had a house listed on St. Anton for $25,999,000. Want to get a good look at one of these waterfront mansions from the street? Good luck – most of them are behind gates, or on heavily treed lots with "No Trespassing" signs. Since most of these places are unlikely to have public open houses if they ever go on the market, your best chance for a peek at Whistler's high-priced lakefront properties is from the small pier at Rainbow Park, across the water from these beachfront palaces.

The St. Anton property, which is named *Arc-en-Ciel*, or "rainbow," was described in the real estate listing as "French-inspired residence on Alta Lake, bordered by a lakefront park." It comes with 260-feet of shoreline, which will come in handy to launch your gold-plated paddle board, and it has stunning mountain and lake views. It includes things you wouldn't find in most homes, like a restored English Pub dating back to the 1830s and now the home's bar, and a monumental pharmacy cabinet used in Paris for 100 years, which is now in the home's kitchen. To spot this manse, you'll need your binoculars. Look for a large white gazebo in front of the house up on the hill. It's right behind the dock, where the owners proudly fly the Canadian Maple Leaf flag.

Address Rainbow Park is at 5778 Alta Lake Road, Whistler, BC V0N 0A0, www.whistler.ca/culture-recreation/parks/rainbow-park | **Getting there** From the Sea to Sky Highway, take the Alta Lake Road exit and follow its winding way along the Valley Trail for about 4 kilometres (2.5 miles). | **Hours** Unrestricted | **Tip** There is so much more to see once you get into a canoe on Alta Lake, the Crown Jewel of Whistler summer recreation. Whistler Eco Tours rents canoes from their Wayside Park location at the South end of Alta Lake (2701 Highway 99, www.whistlerecotours.com).

78   Rebagliati Park
Don't bogart that gold medal, my friend

Here's a question for you: is this park's namesake more famous for winning the first ever snowboarding gold medal at the 1998 Nagano Olympics, or for temporarily losing it over IOC anti-doping allegations of marijuana traces detected in his system? Actually, who cares? Rebagliati Park is a beautiful place to enjoy a coffee, read a good book, or share time with a friend. The story of the local hometown boy who "done good" is worth knowing though.

Ross is actually originally from Vancouver, where he went to Lord Byng High School. But he learned to snowboard and trained in Whistler. After the original IOC disqualification decision was overturned and Ross got his medal back, he instantly became an international media sensation. The next day he appeared on *The Tonight Show* with Jay Leno. Since then, Ross has become a cultural icon in the world of cannabis. He launched a medical marijuana company called Ross's Gold in 2013. Since then, he has branched out into marketing hemp CBD edibles. In October 2013, he was featured on the cover of *High Times* magazine. *The New York Times* ran an article on Ross in November 2018 and quoted him as saying he was happy that marijuana was losing its stigma, even in the world of sports. "Athletes love cannabis because, among other things, it improves concentration and is fat-free and calorie-free," he told the *Times*. Today, Ross lives in Kelowna, BC with his wife and three kids.

The little Park named after Ross is as close to perfect as you can get. Don't expect a lot of amenities though. It only has one bench, and a feature that really grabs your attention is a large, overbuilt, wooden structure without a roof. To get to Rebagliati Park from the Village you pass over Fitzsimmons Creek on a wooden covered bridge. The beautiful relaxing sound of the creek that you can hear in the park is enough to give you a natural high.

Address 4540 Blackcomb Way, Whistler, BC V0N 1B4, www.whistler.ca/culture-recreation/parks/rebagliati-park | Getting there From the Sea to Sky Highway, take the Village Gate exit and turn left on Blackcomb Way, then park at first right. | Hours Unrestricted | Tip Nearby you will find Castros Cuban Cigar Store. They have a good supply of rolling papers (4433 Sundial Place, No. 4, www.getcubans.com).

79 Re-Build-It Center

A fence made of recycled skis

Can you think of a better, more fitting name for a light industrial neighbourhood than Function Junction? Located 10 minutes south of the Village, Function Junction has been around since the early days of Whistler and served the locals with, well, "functional" goods and services. The hardware store, locksmith, and mechanical repair shops are all still there, but today they are mixed in with a new eclectic collection of bakeries, breweries, and bike shops.

One of the more interesting mainstays there for the past 20 years has been the Re-Build-It Center, a thrift store where treasures arrive daily. The store does a brisk trade in used skis. Some of those skis must have come in as singles, were too mangled to re-sell, or just too old to be in demand. All the rejects have ended up on a long, colorful, fence surrounding the second-hand store. Walking along the fence admiring the old relics is like taking a trip through skiing history. You'll find every style, trend and innovation the ski industry has had to offer over the last 50 years nailed to a post on this funny fence – thin, wide, short, long, shaped, and unshaped.

After admiring the skis, step inside for some savings on used clothing, housewares, furniture and of course sports equipment. Legendary stories abound of affluent skiers from overseas coming to Whistler for a week, kitting themselves out with brand new expensive equipment and sportswear – with no intention of taking any of it home. For the super wealthy elite, dropping their stuff off at the Re-Build-It Center after an amazing ski vacation can be easier than packing it for a long flight. Must be nice!

Every day, over a ton of stuff is diverted from the landfill and sold through this non-profit. The money raised from the Re-Build-It Center goes to the Whistler Community Services Society, whose mission is to support and advocate for a healthy community.

Address 1003 Lynham Road, Whistler, BC V0N 1B1, +1 (604) 932-1125, www.mywcss.org/
social-enterprises/re-build-it-centre, rebuildit@mywcss.org | Getting there From the Sea to
Sky Highway, exit onto Alpha Lake Road, then turn right onto Lynham Road. | Hours
Daily 10am – 6pm | Tip If the Function Junction store doesn't have your size or what you
are looking for check out their sister store, the Re-Use-It Centre (8000 Nesters Road,
www.mywcss.org/social-enterprises/re-use-it-centre).

80__The Rembrandt of Snow

Great art hiding in plain sight

Are they trail maps meant to prevent you from getting lost on the mountain, or are they large, framed reproductions of beautiful watercolor paintings meant to be admired by skiers and boarders whizzing by them on the slopes? The amazing colorful maps, painted by the legendary artist and cartographer James Niehues, are both.

It takes a special eye, a steady hand and a very creative mind to take a massive, three-dimensional pair of mountains like Whistler and Blackcomb and accurately depict them on a two-dimensional, flat surface. In today's digital world, Niehues maintains his analog style, hand painting every tree, rock, bump, chairlift, and cliff in such amazing detail that the maps can be trusted to help you navigate both the marked and unmarked areas of Whistler and Blackcomb.

Niehues has been painting these maps for resorts around the world since 1983. He has created hundreds of them and has even been inducted into the United States Ski and Snowboard Hall of Fame. He paints for several Canadian mountains now, but the first one he was commissioned to do was Whistler Blackcomb in 1992. He repainted that map in 1998, and it is the basis of the map you see today on the slopes. Niehues feels a painting is better than a photograph when it comes to ski trails because of the flexibility the artist has to draw directions to individual slopes.

Niehues was recovering from an illness in grade nine, when his mother bought him an oil painting set to help him pass time. Clearly, he has come a long way since then. Today, he is one of the most sought-after and best ski map painters in the world. He recently published his own book. So the next time you are carving a turn on the mountain near one of his art charts, pause, double check that the lighting on it is perfect, and take a few minutes to admire the work of the Rembrandt of Snow.

Address Map signs are all over the mountain, and the large one (pictured) is just outside of the roundhouse at the top of Whistler. | **Getting there** Take the Creekside Gondola or the Village Gondola. | **Hours** Unrestricted | **Tip** James Niehues has just released a new coffee table book called *The Man Behind the Maps*, for sale at the base of Whistler Creekside at Get the Goods (2063 Lake Placid Road, No. 203, www.shop.getthegoods.ca). Or order your copy directly from the artist at www.jamesniehues.com.

81 Rimrock Café
Simply the best

Ask any local where's the most romantic spot in Whistler for a meal. Ask any Whistler hotel concierge what ONE restaurant they recommend to their high-end, fussy international guests from France. Finally, ask a Whistler historian where the town's most established fine dining is. They will all come up with the same answer: the Rimrock Café. It's quite simply the best restaurant in Whistler. Plus the Blue Cheese Iceberg Salad tastes so good it will knock your socks off.

Aside from the amazing food, there are many other factors that make this place interesting and a bit off beat and a true find. The first is its unassuming, understated, lower rent location. The Creekside area is not exactly where the elite meet to eat – most of the fancy restaurants are four klometres (2.5 miles) up the road in the posh Whistler Village. Located off the highway behind some overgrown bushes and big shadowy trees, the Rim Rock Café resides in an old grey wood clad building with a utilitarian look more suitable for a ski shop or youth hostel. There's no fancy lobby, just some modest stairs leading up to epicurean heaven. Before ascending those stairs check out a wall covered in more framed awards, competition certificates, and gourmet citations than you can shake a steamed, lightly buttered asparagus stick at.

It's pricey – and worth every penny. Start with raw oysters, and then sink your teeth into a venison steak with house-made spaetzle, red wine demi-glace, and porcini cream sauce. For dessert, try the crème brulée and a lovely glass of ice wine made in BC.

The service on that second level is world-class. The staff have all worked there for a long, long time and their attention to detail from the moment you arrive is impressive. The Rimrock's co-owner Bob Dawson's story is a familiar one. He came out to Whistler as a skier in 1976, opened the restaurant in 1986, and never looked back.

Address 2117 Whistler Road, Whistler, BC V0N 1B2, +1 (604) 932-5565, www.rimrockcafe.com, info@rimrockwhistler.com | **Getting there** From the Sea to Sky Highway, take the Whistler Road exit. | **Hours** Daily 5:30–9pm | **Tip** Just down the road is another spectacular epicurean delight, the Red Door Bistro. Ask for a seat at the bar so you can watch them prepare your meal (2129 Lake Placid Road, www.reddoorbistro.ca).

82 River of Golden Dreams

Under the sky of love

Usually people write songs about rivers – Blue Danube, Moon River, Whiskey River – but here's a river named after a song. Whistler's River of Golden Dreams is named after the song *Down the River of Golden Dreams*, made popular by The Boswell Sisters in the 1930s. That would be about the time that Alex and Myrtle Philip's Alta Lake getaway Rainbow Lodge was hitting its prime (see ch. 66).

The Boswell Sisters were big radio stars in the 1930s. The story goes that Alex Philip used to paddle honeymooners and lovey-doveys down the river that connects Alta Lake with Green Lake at sunset and croon the words of the song: "Down the river of golden dreams / Just you and I, under the sky of love / And when we find the river's end / Where the willows bend / There our days we'll spend together."

Today you can paddle yourself down the river of golden dreams. And you can sing any song you like. The trip is 3 kilometres (1.8 miles) as the crow flies but 5 kilometres (3 miles) as the paddler paddles. As you voyage down the glacial river's lazy twists and turns, you'll see water lilies, bulrushes, beavers, otters, mink, eagles, ducks, and geese. Maybe even a bear. The scenic route will take you under a railway track, a footbridge, and one or two trees that lean over the water.

You can take the trip a few different ways: sit in an inner tube and let the current do the work; transport and paddle your own canoe; rent a canoe; or take a guided tour. Backroads Whistler and Whistler Eco Tours both offer rentals and packages that give you everything you need, from canoe to paddles to knowledgeable naturalists, that will make your river romp a fun and memorable adventure. Whether you're looking for romance "under the sky of love" or just looking to pass a few hours on the water, the River of Golden Dreams will leave you bewitched and inspired by the natural beauty of this winding watery wonderland.

Address If taking your own canoe, start from Rainbow Park, 5778 Alta Lake Road, Whistler, BC V0N 1B5, www.whistler.ca/culture-recreation/parks/rainbow-park | Getting there From the Sea to Sky Highway, take the Alta Lake Road exit and follow its winding way for about 4 kilometres (2.5 miles). | Hours Unrestricted | Tip The river runs right past Meadow Park, a scenic and serene place for a picnic, and it also has a great playground for kids (Meadow Lane, www.whistler.ca/culture-recreation/parks/meadow-park).

83 Rocks and Gems Canada

How much is that cave bear in the window?

A 40,000-year-old cave bear is the last thing you would expect to see in the upscale and modern Whistler Village. This extraordinary fossilized monster would seem more at home at the American Museum of Natural History in New York City. But no, the daunting, bony creature is right here in the heart of the Village, in the window of a store called Rocks and Gems Canada. It's perched motionless, frozen in time. And here's the best part: it's a real fossilized cave bear.

Its scientific name is *Ursus spelaeus*, and remains of these magnificent creatures can still be found in the mountains of Austria, Romania, and Russia. This one in the store window is slightly crouched, but when in attack mode with its body extended, its height reaches about 3.6 metres (12 feet). So other than captivating tourists passing by, just what is it doing in the window?

You first need to understand that Rocks and Gems is unlike any store you have ever visited. As their name implies, they sell all sorts of rocks, gems, and fossils. They even sell ancient cave bear teeth. With over 650 square metres (7,000 square feet) of display space, no stone is left unturned. They have tons of mineral specimens, semi-precious stones, petrified wood, and fossil jewellery. Add stone carvings, and you get a rock shop like no other. Fossils have been a huge part of the store's identity from their start, and you would be hard pressed to find a better selection of them anywhere in the world. The owners of the store have over 40 years of experience in the business. They know all of their suppliers personally, so there is absolutely no question as to the authenticity of the fossils. Many of the people they source from also supply universities and museums with fossils.

And the answer to the question above is $39,995. Yes, the giant cave bear is indeed for sale. It's the perfect accessory for any caveman's man cave back home.

Address 4154 Village Green, Whistler, BC V8E 1H1, +1 (604) 938-3307, www.rocksandgemscanada.com | Getting there From the Sea to Sky Highway, exit onto Whistler Way, turn right onto Village Green. | Hours Daily 9am–9pm | Tip If after coming out of your "cave" you can't "bear" not having the latest and hottest sporty fashions then head directly to Lulu Lemon's signature store at Whistler, just a few steps away (4154 Village Green, No. 118, www.shop.lululemon.com/stores/ca/whistler/mountainsquare).

84 Royals on Blueberry Hill

All the beds are king-sized

Cast your mind back to 1998. Single dad Prince Charles, recently divorced from Princess Diana, brings his young sons William (age 16) and Harry (age 14) to Whistler for a few days of dad-and-lad adventure on the slopes. Apparently, he had decided the time had come to introduce the princes to Canada and determined that a skiing trip would be the best way to do it. However, there is no palace in Whistler. Not even a castle. So where to stay? The answer was the Blueberry Hill neighborhood, specifically, a four-bedroom home on a very private 993-square-metre (10,689-square-foot) property with spectacular views, and where all the beds are king-sized. The home, a short distance from Whistler Village and Alta Lake, was only a few years old when the three princes moved in, with every modern convenience.

The four-day skiing vacation, the boys' first official trip abroad after Diana's death, followed a 24-hour visit to Vancouver that captivated hundreds of journalists and bedazzled thousands of screaming, swooning girls. The teen princes did their best to act calm in the midst of Beatlesque hysteria as they visited the Michael J. Fox Theatre at Burnaby South Secondary School and, later, the H. R. MacMillan Space Centre in Kitsilano. But they wisely wrapped up their whirlwind visit by hopping on a helicopter and flying to Whistler. Royal watchers on the slopes reported that Charles and the princes tackled all the terrain with skill and confidence.

British Columbia clearly left a strong impression on the two princes, as both have come back as adults. Prince William returned to visit in 2016 with Princess Kate and their two young children along for the tour. Prince Harry returned in 2020 with Meghan and baby Archie before settling in sunny Los Angeles. You can wander around the neighborhood and stop for a selfie in front of the house where three princes once stayed.

Address 3232 Peak Drive, Whistler, BC V0N 1B3 | **Getting there** From the Sea to Sky Highway, exit onto Blueberry Drive, and turn left onto Peak Drive. | **Hours** Viewable from the outside only | **Tip** Blueberry Park, accessible via the Blueberry Trail, has a public dock, regal views, and privacy galore. Go back down Blueberry Drive and turn right on St. Anton Way to the end of the short road, and look for the trail sign (www.trailforks.com/trails/blueberry).

85 Salish Welcome Figure

An ancient welcome

For thousands of years, *Welcome Figures* have been a traditional carving style of the Squamish and Lil'wat Peoples and other Coast Salish communities. These carvings are meant to welcome friends and loved ones onto their shared lands. Out of respect, visitors would wait near them to be welcomed into someone else's territory. Whistler rests within the traditional territory of the Squamish and Lil'wat First Nations. The tall, grey *Welcome Figure Pole* near the Doug Forseth Peak to Peak building on Whistler Mountain is a meaningful, beautiful, and striking marker. Its symbolism becomes even more significant when you think about how the mountain welcomes people from dozens of different countries every year.

How this landmark got here and its true meaning are worth knowing. In 2010, the Whistler Blackcomb Foundation presented a yellow cedar tree harvested from the base of the Symphony Bowl to the Squamish Lil'wat Cultural Center (see ch. 94). Squamish Nation Master Carver Xwalacktun (Rick Harry), his son James, and two other carvers were commissioned to create the figure. People from all over the world spoke with the carvers during the two months they were at the Centre working on the pole.

Step back so that you can admire the figure's four different elements. On the top of the pole is a man with outstretched arms, welcoming friends and loved ones into the territory. Look for the marmot below the man. The marmot is a small indigenous ground squirrel that whistles and inspired the name Whistler (see ch. 110). On the bottom of the pole is a frog, which is a symbol of transition because it can live on land and in the water. If you get a bit closer and look carefully at the carving, you will see individual handprints all around it. These are the hands of all the people who assisted with the carving and a symbol that we are all connected. Welcome to Whistler!

Address The top of Whistler Mountain, Whistler, BC V0N 1B4, close to the entrance to the Roundhouse Lodge, www.whistler.ca/tour/154 | Getting there Take the Creekside Gondola or the Village Gondola. | Hours Unrestricted | Tip Back in town, outside the Audain Art Museum, you'll see a giant aluminum sculpture called *He-yay meymuy* (*Big Flood*), also by Squamish Nation artist Xwalacktun (4350 Blackcomb Way).

86 SAM the Axe Man
Reformed roadside hipster

Driving north along the Sea to Sky Highway, just 2 kilometres (1.25 miles) past the Sea to Sky Gondola, you'll encounter a giant sculpture called SAM, which also stands for "Squamish Axe Man." It's one of those roadside wonders that amuse and delight road trippers as much as they puzzle and confound.

If SAM looks familiar, that could be because it reminds you of the big "Welcome to Brainerd" statue of Paul Bunyan featured in the Netflix series *Fargo*. Or maybe it reminds you of the equally iconic Bunyan statue outside Bemidji, created in 1937. In any case, seeing it will give older travellers a flashback to the days when family road trips were peppered with unusual statues designed to entice, entertain, and inform.

No surprise then to learn that this friendly giant was created as a prop for the 2005 Ice Cube road trip movie *Are We There Yet?*. The movie was partially filmed in the Britannia Beach (see ch. 17) area, and SAM was created by Nick Tattersfield, a local expert at creating monumental sculptures and movie set pieces.

When the filming was over, the axe-wielding wonder left showbiz and made his way to Squamish for a second career as a tourist attraction. He appeared frequently at the Squamish Visitor Information Office, next to the Adventure Centre, and helped promote the annual Squamish Days Loggers Sports Festival. During the 2010 Olympics SAM even made national headlines by donning his own giant-sized red mittens and patriotic red-and-white maple leaf toque. He was almost permanently removed after the Olympics, as some thought his image passé, but he refused to fade away and got a new gig here outside Chances Casino. He also got a $5,000 makeover replacing his hipster toque with a logger's hardhat, a more rakish moustache, and a new smile revealing a new diamond studded tooth. Now he's a big star again and still loves to pose for pictures.

Address 9000 Valley Drive, Squamish, BC V8B 0B3 | Getting there Driving from the Sea to Sky Highway, exit onto Valley Drive. He's right there. | Hours Unrestricted | Tip A bit farther north along the Sea to Sky Highway, stop at the Squamish Adventure Centre. Made from local cedar with a roof that mimics eagle wings, the centre is a great place to see in its own right and also a great source of local information and ideas (38551 Loggers Lane, www.exploresquamish.com/business/squamish-adventure-centre).

87 — The Scandinave Spa

Hot and cold running water

When it's snowing like crazy, and 10 degrees below zero, do you really want to be outside in your bathing suit? If you're at Whistler's famous Scandinavian Spa, the answer is, "Hell yes!" The extreme contrast between hot and cold is often referred to as Nordic or Scandinavian hydrotherapy. It's the real deal and could be one of the reasons that people from Norway, Sweden, and Denmark live to the ripe old average age of 81. This super healthy, centuries-old relaxation method that originated in Northern Europe can be found tucked away in the mountains of Southern British Columbia – at Whistler.

When you jump from a very hot tub into a very cold tub, your blood pressure rises, and your blood vessels contract. These are good things that actually stimulate your immune system. If you see a few Volvos in the large parking lot of the Scandinavian Spa, with Ikea bags in the back and skis on top, that's because Swedes know that jumping between hot and cold tubs also soothes overworked muscles and aching joints. After a battering day of munching moguls and devouring pow, the spa treatment helps in your recovery so that you can return to the mountain the next day and do it all over again.

Even if you don't ski, the spa is a great place to relax and do nothing and leave the multi-tasking, hectic, stressful world behind. Hydrotherapy treatment also cleans and tightens your skin. The hot temperatures open your pores eliminating toxins, while the coldness firms up the skin on your face, restoring that healthy glow that the Vikings surely had when they were raiding Iceland and Greenland 1,000 years ago.

One important thing to know before you go is that there is no talking allowed. So bring a book and a bathing suit, but don't bring anything else. Definitely don't bring your mobile phone! And don't rush your experience – plan on spending two or three hours there at least. A whole day would be even better.

Address 8010 Mons Road, Whistler, BC V8E 1K7, +1 (888) 935-2423, www.scandinave.com/whistler/en, www.info.whistler@scandinave.com | Getting there From the Sea to Sky Highway, exit onto Spruce Grove Way, turn left onto Mons Road, and look for the Volvos. | Hours See website for hours and appointments | Tip The Meadow Park Sports Centre is open to the public, with a hot tub, steam room, sauna, and pool (8625 BC Highway 99, www.whistler.ca/culture-recreation/facilities/meadow-park-sports-centre).

88_ The Sea to Sky Highway
Paving the way to Olympic dreams

Among the most scenic drives on the West Coast of North America are iconic American stunners such as San Francisco to Big Sur, Portland to Redwood National Park, and Seattle to Chuckanut Drive. Canada's Sea to Sky Highway will be near the top of the list. The 163-kilometres (101-mile) route from Vancouver to Whistler quickly puts you and your car at one with nature.

The unique thing about the drive is its proximity to the ocean and the mountains. You'll see rolling waves out one window, and old-growth forests and majestic snow-capped mountains out the other. There are spectacular places to pull over for incredible views, waterfalls, swimming spots, picnic grounds, and museums. While you are enjoying the scenery, it's easy to forget you're steadily gaining altitude. By the time you make it to Whistler, you will be 670 metres (2,200 feet) above sea level. It wasn't always that way though. There was a time when Highway 99, its official name on roadmaps, was dangerous, frustrating, and slow. With its scary, craggy rock abutments, dangerous hairpin turns, and steep hills, the narrow, old, two-lane road earned the nickname, "The Killer Highway."

That all changed in July of 2003, when the Vancouver 2010 Bid Committee pitched the IOC on hosting the Winter Olympic Games in British Columbia. Most of the Olympic alpine sports, including skiing, biathlon, cross-country skiing, Nordic, bobsled, luge, and skeleton events, would be held in Whistler. A major concern for the voting members of the IOC was the two-hour drive from Vancouver to the mountain and the road's track record of about 200 collisions per year. The plan to upgrade the old cliff highway had been in discussion for decades, but it took winning the Olympics bid to attach a deadline to it and expedite – and finance the project to the tune of $600 million – to upgrade the highway and make it safer.

Address The Sea to Sky Highway runs from West Vancouver to Whistler, Pemberton, and eventually ends at Lillooet. | **Getting there** The Sea to Sky Highway runs from Vancouver to Whistler and beyond. | **Hours** Unrestricted | **Tip** As you drive north on the Sea to Sky Highway, look for the vertical metal fencing covering the steep cliff on your right. It is rock fall netting that captures large falling boulders and allows them to pass safely to the base of the net.

89 Seppo Makinen Sculpture
The legend is lionized on Lost Lake Trail

On the Lost Lake trail, you'll discover a sculpture that commemorates a special person in Whistler's growth as a ski resort. Created by local artist Cristina Nick and unveiled in 2012, the sculpture reflects the life of Seppo Makinen (1928–1999), a local legend who, quite literally, helped shape the mountains around Whistler.

Born in a part of Finland that is now a part of Russia, Seppo moved to Canada in 1953. After working around the Alta Lake area clearing power lines in the early 1960s, Seppo got a gig working on the ski trails for the fledgling Garibaldi Lift Company. With a hand-picked posse who shared experience with an axe, an eye for the terrain, a strong back, no fear of bears, good humour, and a love for the outdoors, Seppo and his crew set about the task of creating the ski runs that would delight and challenge the early ski bums and experts intrigued by this burgeoning new resort destination.

Over the next 20 years he walked, hiked, climbed, and cut his way up and down the trails that thousands enjoy today and, perhaps more importantly, blazed a trail into the heart of the community through his unwavering zest for life. At his peak, the lighthearted logger had a 650-square-metre (7,000 square-foot) log house and entertained guests with the aid of a notorious 14-person hot tub. The last trail Seppo laid down is a 1.2 kilometres (.75-mile) black diamond run on Whistler Mountain fittingly called "Seppo's." When Seppo died in 1999, over 800 people gathered to attend his memorial service at the Whistler Conference Centre.

Artist Christina Nick was a perfect choice for this work commissioned by the Whistler Museum and Archives Society. As a skier, former park ranger, naturalist, art teacher, mountain hiker, and adventurous traveler, she empathised with her subject. The sculpture is made of steel and wood, and it's based on her original sketches.

Address 7400 Fitzsimmons Road, Whistler, BC V0N 1B7, www.crosscountryconnection.ca/lost-lake/passivhaus | **Getting there** The sculpture is located opposite the PassivHaus building on the trail to Lost Lake in the Upper Village. | **Hours** Unrestricted | **Tip** The trail that runs under nearby Lorimer Road is where you can see The Lorimer Bridge Mural. It's just 100 metres (325 feet) east of the Seppo Makinen sculpture (www.whistler.ca/tour/147).

90 Shannon Falls
Hop to it

When you hike up to the falls, you'll find evidence of the falls' lumber past. Here and there are some old growth stumps with visible springboard notches where lumberjacks used to stand and saw away with those ridiculously long saws. It must have been thirsty work. So how fitting that Shannon Falls has a little-known role in British Columbia's beer history. These falls were once owned by Carling O'Keefe, one of Canada's "big three" breweries in the late 1900s. From 1976 to 1982, Carling O'Keefe used the falls' crystal-clear, refreshing mountain water for making beer. And not just any beer. The Shannon Falls water was used in Carling's Heidelberg beer, a Canadian Super-Premium beer, that comes in a very recognisable and very collectable, grenade-shaped bottle.

The falls' beer connection goes back even farther. Way back in 1891, before it was a lumber town, Squamish was a hotbed of hop growers. And the president of the Squamish Valley Hop Company was none other than William Shannon. He and his fellow hop farmers shipped hops down to the US, and even to Britain. And, you guessed it, he's the fellow for whom the falls are named.

Beer history aside, the falls have another claim to fame. With a drop of 335 metres (1,100 feet), Shannon Falls is one of the highest waterfalls in BC and certainly one of the most accessible. You'd have to go to Della Falls on Vancouver Island or to Takakkaw Falls in Yoho National Park to find taller falls. So while it may not be the tallest waterfall in the province, it's certainly the one that you have absolutely no excuse for not seeing. Located just a few steps from the Sea to Sky Highway, Shannon Falls is practically a drive thru! If you want a thirst-inspiring workout and awe-inspiring views, continue past the falls on the Sea to Summit trail and take another hike up to the Summit Lodge. Then reward yourself with a local craft beer.

Address The falls are located just off of Highway 99, 2 kilometres (1.25 miles) south of Squamish, immediately adjacent to Stawamus Chief Provincial Park, www.bcparks.ca/explore/parkpgs/shannon. | Getting there From the Sea to Sky Highway, exit onto Shannon Falls Road, drive to the parking lot. | Hours Unrestricted | Tip Speaking of hops, why not pull over and visit the farm stand operated by local area Hop Creek Farms (41060 Government Road, www.hopcreekfarms.com).

91 Shoot in the Mountains
Cordite and conservation

If all the peace, tranquility, and serenity of the mountains just becomes too overwhelming, and you feel the urge to reconnect with the explosive power of human ingenuity, there's a place you can go to make some noise and kick up some dirt: Whistler Shooting Adventures.

Located a short 20-minute drive north of town, the team at the shooting range will hook you up with anything from a dainty pink handgun to an impressive, tripod-mounted rifle with full scope. From low-calibre to large, from handgun to shotgun, they have something for every appetite and every skill level. And, instead of the paper targets you usually get at indoor ranges, they use metal targets that move and make a very satisfying "clang" sound when your round makes contact.

The range is owned by the Pemberton Wildlife Association (PWA), an organization dedicated to wildlife and conservation since 1962, and has been known to locals and law enforcement professionals for some time. Military and police security forces practiced here during the 2010 Olympics, and local RCMP officers still use the range today.

The idea for a pay-to-shoot business came about naturally: many visitors to Whistler wanted a place to try some recreational shooting, and the Wildlife Association wanted revenue to fund its various conservation projects. PWA member Clark Gatehouse created Whistler Shooting Adventures in 2014 to see if there was a way to make it work for everyone. It was a good call.

All kinds of people are now enjoying the experience of shooting at the range – men women, locals, visitors, certain unnamed members of certain royal families, the occasional Hollywood celebrity, some members of some professional sports teams you might know. And demand is strong enough that the range stays open all year long. Recently, Clark was able to give the Wildlife Association a $10,000 donation to help purchase a wetlands area in Pemberton.

Address Sea to Sky Highway, Pemberton, BC V0N 2L1, +1 (604) 935-8778, www.whistlershooting.com, whistlershooting@gmail.com | **Getting there** From the Sea to Sky Highway going north from Whistler, drive approximately 25 kilometres (15.5 miles), look for the sign on the left that says *Gun Range*. | **Hours** Call for reservations | **Tip** For the full rugged outdoorsman experience, visit or spend the night at nearby Nairn Falls campsite, just another 2 kilometres (1.25 miles) up the highway. The falls are just a short 1.5-kilometre (1-mile) hike from the parking lot (www.bcparks.ca/explore/parkpgs/nairn_falls).

92 The Sitting Man
Say hello to Jeri

The awkward position of *Jeri* has been the source of some juvenile bathroom humor, but it is nevertheless regarded by some to be one of the most outstanding works of public art in all of Whistler. When you first approach the sculpture, typically from behind, it looks like a man squatting behind some bushes. (That's where the potty jokes come in.) But as you get closer and take in the work from its side profile, or from the front, you cannot help but be inspired and moved by the artistic technique of its creator, local artist James Stewart.

Up close, the muscles, veins, and sinews of the man are profoundly detailed and yet also impressionistic. The arms are particularly impressive and seem as though they may belong to a professional basketball player – muscular, long, and powerful yet also graceful. That he appears athletic is no accident.

The sculpture *Jeri* represents an Afro-Brazilian martial arts practitioner resting after his performance of the martial art of *capoeira*. Capoeira blends dance, acrobatics, and music and often involves inverted kicks and hands on the ground. Now that you know that, the sculpted man's posture and expression begin to make sense. Looking at his bald head, bearded chin, and furrowed brow, political scientists might think he looks a bit like Vladimir Lenin (though Lenin was surely never so fit). Sit with *Jeri* and take in the beauty around you.

While the bronze sculpture of *Jeri* is very solid and tactile in the traditional style of sculptures everywhere, James Stewart is also in every way a very modern artist just as comfortable with a handful of clay as with a computer. His background includes some impressive contributions to contemporary film. In Los Angeles, he was lead modeller on *The Chronicles of Narnia*, a modeller on *Shrek*, and a creature supervisor on one of the *Harry Potter* movies, among other impressive artistic achievements.

Address Rebagliati Park, Whistler, BC V0N 1B4, www.artswhistler.com/location/jeri | **Getting there** From Parking Lot 1 at the southwest end of Rebagliati Park, walk east toward the park over Valley Trail. As you approach the covered wooden bridge, look to your right. Jeri's back will be toward you. | **Hours** Unrestricted | **Tip** See more of Stewart's work at the Adele Campbell Fine Art Gallery in the Westin Resort & Spa (4090 Whistler Way, No. 109, www.adelecampbell.com).

93 __ The Southside Diner

Does a duck have two legs or four?

If you had a time machine to transport yourself back to the early heydays of Whistler, your first stop would be the Southside Diner. Back then, the intersection of Highway 99 and Lake Placid Road was the epicenter of what would grow into a vibrant, wild, youth-fueled, and glorious ski culture. In the early 1970s, Whistler was not much more than a big parking lot, the Husky Gas station, a few lift lines and a ski rental shop. The original ski rental shop was in the building that the Southside Diner occupies today.

That building has gone through several commercial iterations since it fitted the long-hairs with skis. It was a deli for a while, then an oyster bar, and in 2004, it became the Southside Diner. Some of that irreverent ski culture from days gone by still exists at the Southside Diner. The first piece of physical evidence is an original, antiquated, two-seat, wooden ski lift chair. It hangs from the awning on top of the wooden stairs outside the restaurant's entrance, and it was part of the "Orange" chair lift that once was one of the main ways to get up the mountain. Within arm's reach from the orange chair is the restaurant's front door, where an old ski has been repurposed to be the handle.

Once inside the cozy 40-seat eatery, you'll notice that the walls are festooned with framed black and white photos depicting the non-stop recreational winter party that Whistler became shortly after opening. Look for the famous 1973 picture taken by photographer Chris Speedie at Toad Hall that shows 14 skiers standing side by side and buck naked. The photo is a celebration of youthful debauchery and captures the spirit of the time!

The Diner has great food, great service, and is full of locals. It's about as authentic as you can possibly get. Try the mouthwatering Three Legged Duck, which is three Crispy Drumettes on a bed of truffle fries and a balsamic reduction drizzle.

Address 2102 Lake Placid Road, Whistler, BC V0N 1B2, +1 (604) 966-0668, www.southsidediner.ca, southsidediner@shaw.ca | Getting there Heading south from Whistler Village on the Sea to Sky Highway, turn right onto Lake Placid Road. Destination is on the corner. | Hours Sun–Wed 8am–4pm, Thu–Sat 8am–9pm | Tip If you are looking for inexpensive lodging in Whistler, the Southside Whistler Center Lodge above the diner has rooms that rent out for between $60 to $90 per night (2102 Lake Placid Road, www.snowboardwhistler.com/southside).

94__ The Squamish Lil'wat Cultural Centre

Indigenous insights

Visit the Squamish Lil'wat Cultural Centre for new perspectives on the Whistler area. The building itself is stunning – an architectural achievement that blends ancient and modern materials. It's both stately and welcoming. But it's inside where you'll really start to connect with the Indigenous peoples who first lived in this area.

The main feature of the centre is its guided "What We Treasure" tour, hosted by the centre's youth ambassadors. Unlike typical tour guides, these ambassadors don't have a routine script memorized or a defined set of facts and details to tell you about the exhibits. Instead, each ambassador is a member of the Lil'wat or Squamish Nation and will give you an interpretation of the artefacts through the lens of their own personal or family experience with it.

The artefacts you'll see include canoes, baskets, traditional clothing, paddles, drums, stone tools, and other items used by the community. Most of these artifacts are relatively new pieces, partially to showcase the craftsmanship of the current generation, but also because so many of the ancient items were confiscated by the government during the potlatch ban (1885–1951). Or their owners destroyed them rather than surrender them to the government.

In the centre's surrounding outdoor area, you can step inside an *istken*, a traditional wooden home built partially underground. You can also go on a guided forest walk. The forest walk takes about an hour and starts with a welcome song by the ambassador.

The centre's Indigenous-inspired Thunderbird Café combines traditional ingredients with a contemporary spin. Try the venison chili with a fresh bannock. The Gift Shop sells items handmade by Squamish, Lil'wat, and other First Nations artists.

Address 4584 Blackcomb Way, Whistler, BC V0N 1B4, +1 (866) 441-7522, www.slcc.ca |
Getting there From the Sea to Sky Highway, exit onto Lorimer Road, then right on
Blackcomb Way. Destination is on your right. | **Hours** See website for hours and events |
Tip Visit the Olympic Plaza to view *Olympic Lightning Figure*, a snake totem carving
by Squamish Nation master carver Ray Natraoro (Sesiysm) and Lil'wat Nation carver
Delmar Williams (Bankscht) (Olympic Plaza: 4365 Blackcomb Way).

95 Sunny Chibas
Watch out for the wrestling chickens

The building is colourful, the theme is extroverted, the concept is bizarre, and the food is delicious! Welcome to Sunny Chibas, the Mexican restaurant run by a French-trained chef inspired by 1990s Bronx rapper Sonny Cheeba and 1970s Japanese martial artist movie superstar Shinichi (Sonny) Chiba. When you drive around the parking area, you'll see an amazing mural of wrestling chickens that also lets you know something unusual is going on. As you approach the front door, you'll see it's peppered with hundreds of stickers and decals. And if you meet owner and head chef Aaron Lawton, you'll notice he is decorated with a pretty impressive set of tattoos too.

This place is where visual design, rap music, Japanese movies, and French cooking collide to produce some of the tastiest Mexican-style food you've ever tasted. It's almost as much a feast for the eyes as it is for the stomach. The fried chicken is sensational, and the chimichangas are always in high demand, but, in addition to quesadillas, enchiladas, burritos, huaraches, tacos, tortas, and nachos, you can also order up a hearty Canadian plate of poutine. The restaurant is a local favourite, and being so close to the highway and its parade of often hungry, often curious travellers, it also welcomes visitors from all over the world.

Like many businesses located in a region where many Hollywood productions are made, it also has the occasional celebrity customer. *Scream* actor and professional wrestler David Arquette dropped by once. Maybe it was the wrestling chickens mural that caught his eye, or maybe it was because he knows Squamish-born UFC fighter Cole ("The Cole Train") Smith likes to build up his strength here when he's not competing in Los Angeles or Thailand.

Sunny Chibas packs a punch, and if you've driven past it too many times before, now is the time to pull over and see what you've been missing. Don't chicken out!

Address 1584 British Columbia 99, Squamish, BC V8B 0H2, +1 (604) 898-1306 | Getting there Heading south on the Sea to Sky Highway, just past the Cleveland Avenue exit for Squamish, continue across the bridge and take the first exit on your right. | Hours Sun–Thu noon–8pm, Fri & Sat noon–9pm | Tip Another great food experience not far from here is the Lebanese restaurant Saha Eatery. Tell them Chef Aron sent you (38128 2nd Avenue, www.sahaeatery.ca).

96 Tall Tree Bakery
Best cinnamon buns this side of the Rockies

The best-tasting cinnamon bun this side of the Rocky Mountains is mere steps away from the Sea to Sky Highway, just past the main turn-offs for Squamish. You've routinely been blasting past the highway's Commercial Way exit in your zeal to get to your destination, but you have been missing out on something special. It's time to slow down and smell the roses. Or in this case, slow down and eat the pastries.

Started in 2016 by wife-and-husband team Erin Copeland and Sean Tremblay, the Tall Tree Bakery is one of the best, most wholesome, bakeries you'll find. It's not glamorous, it's not chic, it's not cosmopolitan, and it's neither pretentious nor conspicuous. All you will get here is some of the best baked goods you've ever had, made by people who believe in what they're doing and believe in doing it well.

Sean starts hours before sunrise to make sure everything is baked fresh from scratch every day. Erin keeps more normal hours and manages the business operations. Working together like sugar and cinnamon, they deliver the goods. The daily bread menu includes staples like French bread, baguettes, croissants, *pan au chocolat*, epi-baguettes, and sourdough breads. But some days, Sean will bake a feature bread, like a cinnamon raisin loaf or rosemary feta honey wheat sourdough. If bagels are your thing, visit on a Wednesday or Sunday. Those are the bagel days. It's hard to choose between a honey lemon cream puff or a peanut butter and jam cream puff, but such are the challenges you'll find here.

Most bakeries will tell you the secret to success is quality ingredients and unique skills of some kind, or perhaps hard work and determination. All that is true here too, but the really rare element is the passion Erin and Sean have for what they do and the opportunity they have to do it together and bring joy to their customers. So this is not just another bakery – it's a dream come true.

Address 1201 Commercial Way, No. 404, Squamish, BC V8B 0V1, +1 (604) 849-0951, www.talltreebakery.com, info@talltreebakery.com | Getting there From the Sea to Sky Highway, take the Commercial Way exit and drive about 0.5 kilometres (0.3 mile) to the intersection with Queen's Way. Turn right, parking on your right. | Hours Wed–Fri 8am–4pm, Sat & Sun 9am–4pm | Tip Tall Tree gets their coffee from Counterpart Coffee nearby. Buy a pound or two of your own to enjoy at home (39012 Discovery Way, No. 107, www.counterpartcoffee.com).

97 __ TNT Tattoo and Barber
Mountains of ink

Many of the finest boutiques and the most accomplished people make their way to Whistler's quaint Upper Village. So it should be no surprise that TNT Tattoo and Barber, the Resort Municipality's top tattoo parlor and barber shop, is located there too, just a short stroll away from the swanky Fairmont Chateau Whistler.

The business was co-founded by two talented guys named Tyler. So Tyler and Tyler became Tyler 'N Tyler, and Tyler 'N Tyler became TNT. It turns out that was not just a convenient moniker for the business but also a prophetic one, as they do things with needles and razors that will blow your mind.

The Tyler who is the creative force behind the tattoo side of things is the one known as TylerATD. And, in case you ever worry about permanently inking your body, the "ATD" stands for "Attention To Detail," which is important for a tattoo artist. He actually started off as a graffiti artist many years ago before becoming a tattoo artist and eventually launching TNT here on Halloween night in 2018.

TylerATD can tattoo pretty much anything but is well known for his work in black and shades of grey. Since this is Whistler, he's naturally no stranger to fishing, skiing, snowboarding, and hiking, so he has a great eye for the natural environment. He has many fans proudly sporting one or more of his fastidiously detailed wolf, bear, eagle, or salmon illustrations on some body part.

You'd think that many people come to Whistler for the skiing or the hiking, and then they decide to get a tattoo while they're here – and you'd be right. But the opposite is also true. Some people travel long distances just to get a quality TNT tattoo and then add on some outdoor adventure after that. Some of TNT's most loyal customers book hotel reservations and tattoo appointments months in advance of their vacations. TNT is the place for a haircut and some mountain ink.

Address 4573 Chateau Boulevard, No. 4, Whistler, BC V0N 1B4, +1 (604) 935-3922, www.tntwhistler.com | **Getting there** From the Sea to Sky Highway, exit onto Village Gate Boulevard, then right onto Blackcomb Way, then right onto Chateau Boulevard. | **Hours** Daily 11am–7pm, call for an appointment | **Tip** If you want to show off your new tattoo, the grand lobby of the Chateau Fairmont Whistler, just steps away, is one of the fanciest places to see and to be seen (4599 Chateau Boulevard, www.fairmont.com/whistler).

98 Treeline Aerial

Hanging out with friends for a secret workout

When you spend some time practising aerial yoga, engaging in pole fitness, or learning static trapeze maneuvers on a silk rope, your mind is so engaged in the activity that your body doesn't even realize it's getting a workout. That's why some call these kinds of activities a "secret workout." Treeline Aerial gives you a unique physical activity unlike any other – sort of like dance, sort of like gymnastics, sort of like CrossFit, sort of like yoga. It's also sort of like being in the circus, which is no surprise really because Treeline founder Dani Duncan got her start teaching circus arts.

Many people enjoy this form of physical activity because it's more performance art than fitness routine. Instructors teach the basic moves and skills, but after that, much of the workout is up to you. It's great for people who want to be physically challenged without having the pressure of having to "win," who like to be engaged in a group activity without having the responsibility of being on a team, and for those who are looking for a peaceful activity that combines mental and physical health in one activity.

The other thing that makes this a secret workout is its location. Getting there feels like you're on a mystery tour. But if you're going to hang silk ropes from a ceiling 6 metres (20 feet) high, then you need to find a very specific type of building for that. And the one that Dani found used to be a welding shop. Fortunately, that just adds to the surprising and delightful experience of finding it for the first time.

Dani and friends have totally renovated the place with colourful silks installed in the main area, workout poles installed in the back area, and hanging yoga equipment in the loft area. The red cedar paneling with its warm tones is recycled from a friend's house. There's padded flooring throughout should you ever wish to get your feet back on the ground. But you'll want to keep flying here.

Address 1330 Alpha Lake Road, No. 103, Whistler, BC V0N 1B1, www.treelineaerialbc.com, info@treelineaerialbc.com | **Getting there** From the Sea to Sky Highway, exit on Alpha Lake Road at Function Junction and follow it for about 700 metres. It'll be on your left. | **Hours** See website for class schedule | **Tip** Treeline instructors say their favourite place to get workout tights and activewear is Bewildher, the eco-friendly, slow-fashion, charitable, Squamish-based online shop (www.bewildher.com). All garments are sewn in a women-owned factory that pays fair wages in Vancouver, BC.

99 Trevor Petersen's Ice Axe

The ultimate alpine accolade

Just below the summit of Blackcomb Mountain, there is an ice axe discretely bolted to the million-year-old granite. It's often covered by snow. At the adze end of the axe is a square sticker with the words, "Trevor Would Do it." On the shaft is the name "Trevor Petersen," and the dates "1962–1996." The axe was placed here shortly after Trevor died in a tragic avalanche in France by his friends and loyal members of a unique brand of mountain daredevils and adventurers.

Memories have faded since 1996, and a whole new generation of extreme athletes has flooded our screens with spectacular GoPro videos and slick media productions. But in those pre-internet days, Petersen was one of the best-known, original, and authentic characters in the niche world of extreme skiing. Through his towering personality, he did much to spread Whistler's reputation around the world.

Together with ski legends like Eric Pehota and Peter "The Swede" Mattsson, Trevor Petersen was among the first to open up the back-country in the Whistler area, skiing many places that previously had only ever been climbed. He was the first to ski Cleverest Couloir off the peak of Blackcomb Mountain (now permanently closed) and, with Pehota and Mattsson, the first to ski in the Tantalus Range, and the first to ski the north face of Mount Fitzsimmons.

From the top of Blackcomb Mountain, you're looking out over some of the best alpine views in the world. You can choose from two hundred marked-off ski runs and over eight thousand acres of terrain, sixteen alpine bowls, and three glaciers.

WARNING: The axe itself is not far from a ski run called, "DOA." So finding it is a challenge best left to experienced mountaineers. Like Trevor's own zest for life, though, this very special memorial axe will inspire you to embrace adventure in your own life, whether you find the axe or just know it's nearby.

Address The top of Blackcomb Mountain, Whistler, BC, www.whistlerblackcomb.com |
Getting there The axe is located not far from a backcountry ski run called "DOA." From
the Glacier Express take the Showcase T-bar. | Hours See website for chairlift schedule |
Tip Visit Toad Hall Studios in Function Junction and ask about their "Trevor Would Do
It" stickers (1365 Alpha Lake Road, No. 6, www.ths.ca).

100__Vallea Lumina

Magic among the mountains

"Legends say there's a hidden valley where the stardust falls from the sky, filling all living things with its pure light." That's what the marketing team at Vallea Lumina will tell you, but some of what they say is actually true. They have created a walk in the woods that's like no trail you've ever been on before. It's a trail with a tale – a forested fantasy that delights your sense of the wondrous and the whimsical.

Tucked away in a magical mountainside, the creators of Vallea Lumina bring Whistler's forest to life each night with a host of special effects matched only in Hollywood movies and the corners of your mind. Created by Montreal's phenomenally successful Moment Factory, the experience combines elements of lighting, sound effects, music, holographic projections, fog machines, and physical elements to create an immersive experience like no other. It's a spectacular and magical 1.5-kilometres (1-mile) hike through an enchanted forest. You can experience the night walks with your kids, or you can do them with your date – it's one of those universal delights that appeals to just about anyone.

The Moment Factory was created in 2001 by Dominic Audet, Sakchin Bessette, and Jason Rodi and was initially conceived as an all-online video art gallery. But the multimedia entertainment studio soon began providing support to clients looking to add memorable moments to their places and events, like creating a media installation for the Los Angeles Airport, an in-cinema opening show for a Sony Pictures screening event, and lighting effects for Nine Inch Nails' "Lights in the Sky" tour, for Madonna, and Celine Dion. Then in 2014 they created the first Lumina experience – an enchanted night walk at Quebec's Parc de la Gorge de Coaticook. People loved it so much that there are now 11 Lumina night walk experiences around the globe, including this one in Whistler.

Address 4293 Mountain Square, No. 211, Whistler, BC V8E 1B8, +1 (833) 800-8480, www.vallealumina.com | Getting there Exit the Sea to Sky Highway at Cougar Mountain Road, a short 10-minute drive from Whistler Village. Park at the base camp. Transportation can be provided, call or visit website for more information. | Hours See website for schedule of events | Tip If magic in the mountains is what you're after, and if you're looking for a nice intermediate mountain bike trail, try the Magic Chair trail on Blackcomb Mountain (www.trailforks.com/trails/magic-chair).

101 Valley Trail
Part of the Trans Canada Trail

If Vancouver's iconic Stanley Park Seawall is Canada's most scenic 10-kilometres (6.2-mile) stroll, then Whistler's Valley Trail is a close second. It's four times as long and quite a bit different, but just as breathtaking, refreshing, and interesting every step of the way.

The Valley Trail connects all of Whistler's neighbourhoods from Function Junction at the south end to Emerald at the north. It passes several lakes, the Village, the Upper Village, and Creekside, and it also goes through many interesting residential areas. It's a safe and easy trail with an even surface – you can even wear your running shoes and leave your hiking boots at home. It also has plenty of interpretative and wayfaring signs and rest stops along the way, and you are never deep in the woods or too far away from a restroom or the Sea to Sky Highway. If you look up the phrase "leisurely pleasant strolls" in the dictionary, a picture of this trail should pop up. And the best thing is you can easily bite off short, medium, and longer chunks of it depending on your time schedule or fitness level.

Where the Valley Trail has Stanley Park beat is in the number of eclectic, beautiful pieces of art that you will encounter along the way. The municipality of Whistler publishes a comprehensive little pocket guide of all the 157 public works of art scattered throughout the entire Whistler region; 25 of these are on the Valley Trail. You can get the free 20-page guide and map booklet at the Municipal Hall or at many of the tourist information kiosks throughout Whistler. Keep your eye out for the world's largest pine cone sculpture, a couple of giant Adirondack chairs, and the eclectic *Three Ravens* sculpture perched above the pathway.

After completing the trail, if you're inspired to walk all the way across Canada, then you'll be glad to know that Whistler's Valley Trail is actually part of the Trans Canada Trail.

Address The Valley Trail runs throughout the Whistler area and is accessible from several different locations, www.whistler.com/activities/valley-trail | **Getting there** From Function Junction at the most southerly access, look for the trail access at the end of Lynham Road. | **Hours** Unrestricted | **Tip** Never go for a hike without carrying a water bottle. The Whistler Home Hardware store is at the beginning of the trail at Function Junction and has a nice variety to choose from (1005 Alpha Lake Road, www.homehardware.ca/en/store/51661).

102 Walk the Snow Walls

World's largest open-air refrigerator

If you time it just right, you can visit a special place that's only there part of the year. It's partly created by nature and partly created by machine. It's a unique phenomenon known as the Snow Walls. The walls are created in the early summer months as snow from the previous winter begins to melt and the snowplows from Whistler Blackcomb clear a path for maintenance vehicles to access the top of the Peak Chair. When you walk along this remarkable path, formed annually in a silent partnership between machine and nature, the experience of walking between giant walls of snow, surrounded in light, is almost meditative.

Start your epic trek from the Whistler Village by taking a gondola ride up to the Roundhouse Lodge. From there, follow the signs for Pika's Traverse. Follow that uphill about 2.3 kilometres (1.4 miles) until you reach Matthew's Traverse Road. This is where you'll find a premium Snow Wall experience. Hike a further .9 kilometres (.6 mile) along Matthews's Traverse to the Top of The World Summit and be rewarded with more spectacular views, including one of the most famous and most photographed Inukshuks in the world (see ch. 47).

Timing your visit is a little tricky. If you go in May, you'll have to do more walking because the Peak Express chairlift may not be open to take you back down to the Roundhouse. But if you go in June when the lift is open, the snow walls may not be as impressive due to melting.

Whenever you decide to go, make sure you're dressed for the trip. You can get away with wearing shorts and a t-shirt, but don't think you can get away with just that. Pack a few extra layers in case (when) things begin to get chilly. It's like walking through the world's longest open-air refrigerator. Comfortable hiking shoes are best, but running shoes will do. It's not a difficult hike, but it is a bit rocky, and you'll need to watch where you're going.

Address Creekside or Village Gondolas, Whistler, BC V0N, www.whistlerblackcomb.com |
Getting there Take the Creekside Gondola or the Village Gondola to the Roundhouse. Follow
the signs for Pika's Trail. | **Hours** Seasonal, best seen late May–mid-June. Check website for
gondola hours. | **Tip** Everything you need for your alpine adventures, from sunglasses to
backpacks, can be found at McCoo's (4293 Mountains Square, www.mcooswhistler.ca).

103 The Waterfall House

A river runs through it

Built in 2005, this palatial Panorama Ridge pad, locally known as the Waterfall House but actually named Stonecliff Falls, has a waterfall flowing next to the garage. For that feature alone, this house is a place in Whistler that you will not want to miss.

Considered an architectural and design masterpiece, the home has four bedrooms and just under 465 square metres (5,000 square feet) of living space spread out over six towering stories. And it features spectacular views of Alta Lake and the mountains beyond – Sproatt, Mount Currie, and Whistler, and Blackcomb. This iconic Whistler residence was designed by Vancouver architect John Dow Medland, but owner local real estate mogul Viive Truu poured years of luxury home experience into the design and is responsible for many of the most gushed-over features. Those lucky enough to see the inside, report that the interior glows in the warmth of Nigerian hardwood, Australian walnut, and European beechwood. Exotic stuff for sure, but Truu also wanted a West Coast vibe in some places, so she had old-growth fir logs imported from Vancouver Island to provide just the right touch. Vancouver glass artist Yves Trudeau was recruited to help create an indoor glass-and-stainless-steel waterfall installation. There's caramel-colored rock in the spa room.

While the interior is something only the fortunate few behold, most people are satisfied just to get the curbside view, looking up at the towering cliffs and rocks from the street below. When you take in the raw, rocky exterior melting into the landscape above, you'll be amazed and bewildered. But be sure to smile because there are at least 15 security cameras looking right back!

The average price for a single family home in Whistler these days hovers somewhere around $3M, but if you want to live in a place like this you'll need a river of cash or a mountain-sized mortgage.

Address 3350 Panorama Ridge, Stonecliff Falls, Whistler, BC V8E 0W1 | Getting there From the Sea to Sky Highway, take the Panorama Ridge exit. | Hours Viewable from the outside only | Tip Take a hike to a real waterfall – Rainbow Falls is just 1 kilometre (0.6 mile) in along the Rainbow Lake Trail to Rainbow Lake, where Whistler's water comes from. The trail itself is a pleasant 16-kilometres round trip that can be done in under six hours (www.alltrails.com/trail/canada/british-columbia/rainbow-lake-trail).

104_ The West Coast Railway Heritage Park

Western Canada's largest collection of rolling stock

Did you ever dine at Le Railcar Restaurant in Vancouver's Gastown District in the 1970s? Ever wonder what happened to it? According to Trainweb.org, the last restaurant there went bankrupt in 2002. But the actual train car is right here at the West Coast Railway Heritage Park. It's been fully restored to its origins as Canadian Pacific Railway Business Car #8, or The Alberta Railcar. This unique piece of railway history, built in 1929, was one of 10 business cars, each named after a Canadian province.

When you come to the 4-hectare (12-acre) West Coast Railway Heritage Park, take your time and be prepared to walk – a lot. Visiting the largest collection of railway rolling stock in Western Canada and the second largest collection of vintage locomotives nationwide, you will enjoy all sorts of interesting surprises and curiosities. Don't miss the British Columbia Business Car (the oldest in the collection and dating to 1890), a rare Canadian Pacific Colonist Sleeping Car from 1905, the only authentic Railway Post Office Car in Canada, various cabooses, an actual train station, and even a railway roundhouse.

Not all of the objects here are trains. There's a 1937 Ford V8 sedan, nicknamed the "Grey Ghost," which once rode the rails as a Pacific Great Eastern Railway inspection car. The majestic metal monster had a bell hanging from its front fender to proclaim its presence, and flanges were mounted behind the wheels so it could switch from road to rail in a jiffy. There's a tribute of sorts to Billy Miner, Canada's first train robber, and the noted "gentleman bandit," who coined the phrase, "Hands up!" Young visitors will appreciate the Miniature Railway, the annual Thomas the Tank Engine event, and a holiday ride on The Polar Express.

Address 39645 Government Road, Squamish, BC V8B 0B6, +1 (604) 898-9336, www.wcra.org | Getting there From the Sea to Sky Highway, exit onto Industrial Way to the intersection at Queens Way. Turn right and follow the signs. | Hours See website for seasonal hours | Tip If you like exploring engines of yesteryear, make a whistle stop at Brennan Park Recreation Centre and see some of the old logging equipment outside (1009 Centennial Way, www.squamish.ca/rec/recreation-facilities/brennan-park-recreation-centre).

105 Whiskey Jack Birds
Actually, they're gray jays

At the bottom of Whistler's Harmony Chair, you can be certain of three things: there will be a line-up, the liftee will have an Australian accent, and there will be lots of Whiskey Jack birds descending on people's helmets, hands, and outstretched ski poles. It's a very charming and utterly Whistler experience.

But what is it about that particular lift, of all the lifts at Whistler, that attracts these cute little birds? Part of it has to do with the concession stand near the chair. Whiskey Jacks are always scavenging for small morsels of food on the ground, so hanging out by a snack shack only makes sense. They also feel comfortable in clearings near a forest, which pretty much describes the bottom of the Harmony Chair. Finally, through the years, these smart little birds have trained skiers to feed them, and the long line ups that form at that particular chair assure fertile feeding. As the sign very clearly points out in the lift line-up, feeding human food to birds is not good for them, so remember to bring bird seed.

The Whiskey Jack's real name is Gray Jay, but almost no one refers to them by that name at Whistler. The Whiskey Jack moniker is actually the anglicized version of the Cree word *Wisakedjak*. That makes the Gray Jay Canada's only bird mostly referred to by a traditional Indigenous name. The Cree language is spoken across a huge region of Canada and the United States and legend has it that Wisakedjak was a benevolent and humorous character and a cultural hero of the Cree tribe. He was a bit of a trickster too and like the birds at Whistler, he was a friend of humankind and was never portrayed in a dangerous manner. So don't be afraid of these little birds while you are in the ski line up – just relax and observe them. You may learn something because some Cree legends state that the great Spirit created Wisakedjak to be a teacher of humankind.

Address At the top of Whistler Mountain, Whistler, BC V0N 1B4 | Getting there Take the Creekside Gondola or the Village Gondola. You will need a trail map to direct you to the bottom of the Harmony chair. | Hours Unrestricted | Tip The signs at the bottom of the lift tell you not to feed the birds. Our human food is not good for them. Bird seed on the other hand is more appealing to the avian palate and healthy for them too. Whistler Happy Pets sells it (1085 Millar Creek Road, No. 101, www.whistlerhappypets.com).

106_Whistler Hardware

If I had a hammer, I'd still come here for nails

Shane Holland, the owner of Whistler Hardware, considers himself the store's eclectic curator, responsible for carefully selecting each and every one of the 14,000 unique items for sale in the Village's oldest store. The place is worth a visit just to see how it is physically possible to cram so many brand-new, shiny whatcha-ma-call-its, thing-a-ma-bobs, and doo-dads into this local hardware store. It's also worth visiting to help you truly appreciate the tremendous construction boom Whistler has experienced since the humble and hearty hardware store opened in 1980.

They say location is everything when it comes to real estate, and this trailblazing store was truly in the right place at the right time. Imagine the Whistler Village back then as basically a giant construction site, with buildings popping up like mushrooms. Each construction project required assorted hardware, plumbing, electric, and building supplies, and the builders could save themselves a trip to Squamish by simply walking to the newly opened Whistler Hardware. In many ways the store helped build Whistler.

Today, the old-fashioned, jam-packed hardware retailer almost seems out of place surrounded by all sorts of sophisticated clothing stores, boutiques, and restaurants. The clientele has also become more diversified since the days when most of the customers wore steel-toed boots and construction hats. Whistler Hardware customers today fall into four categories: guests staying in nearby hotels that forgot to pack something, condo owners visiting for the weekend intent on making some quick repairs, Whistler Village building maintenance workers, and still the occasional construction worker. In some ways the store has changed very little over the years. It's quite an experience to walk into a hardware store of old, a throwback of a place that has everything you need, even if you didn't know you need it.

Address 4305 Village Stroll, No. 101, Whistler, BC V8E 1E4, +1 (604) 932-3863, www.whistlerhardware.ca | **Getting there** From the Sea to Sky Highway, exit onto Village Gate Boulevard and follow it to the intersection with Blackcomb Way. Village Stroll is a short walk east of the parking lots. | **Hours** Mon–Thu 9am–6pm, Fri & Sat 9am–8pm, Sun & holidays 10am–5:30pm | **Tip** Right next door is a great little delicatessen named after the owner Ingrid. She makes a tasty schnitzel sandwich (4305 Skiers Approach Road, www.ingridswhistler.com).

107__ The Whistler Hat Gallery
Everything from toques to trilbys

Don't let the friendly and knowledgeable staff at The Whistler Hat Gallery pull the wool over your eyes when you drop into their charming little store in the Village. Brushing up on your cap knowledge before going inside is easy to do by just quickly looking at the detailed-yet-simple, black-and-white hat chart posted in the front window.

Did you know there are over 24 different, easily identified, distinct styles of hats? Here are a few you may have heard of: Aviator, Ten Gallon, Trapper, Baseball, Beanie, and Bowler. Then there are the more obscure ones that you may not be familiar with, like Ascot, Pork Pie, Deerstalker, Boater, and Greek Fisherman. There aren't many styles of hats that the Whistler Hat Gallery doesn't have in stock. They bring them in from all over the world. From the dusty Australian plains, they import Outback hats, and from the stylish sophisticated streets of Manhattan, they bring in Fedoras. They even have a great selection of made in Canada: grab-and-go Toques. Looking for a Mountie hat? …well you get the picture.

What kind of people shop at the Whistler Hat Gallery? You'd expect scatterbrained skiers who forgot to pack a toque to be a large part of their business, and they are. But the store also has a steady stream of perennial global customers who make a habit of coming back year after year to add a new lid to their growing collection, souvenirs of their visits to Whistler. In terms of the split between winter and summer hat sales, it's about 50/50.

In case you're wondering just what a Pork Pie hat is, here is the clever description that accompanies its illustration on the window chart. "If you're a chemistry teacher who's found a new calling cooking meth, this is the hat for you." And the Greek Fisherman hat? "It's often worn by single Australian surfers, who are doing their best to go home with you." Clearly, there's a hat for everyone.

Address 4295 Blackcomb Way, No. 103 B, Whistler, BC V8E 0X2, +1 (604) 938-6695, www.whistlerhatgallery.com | Getting there From the Sea to Sky Highway, exit onto Village Gate Boulevard, turn right, and park. | Hours Daily 10am–10pm | Tip Leaving the store, turn left and walk toward the central plaza. That's where you'll find a beautiful, tall, wooden *Welcoming Figure*. The lead carver was Tawx'sin Yexwulla, Poolxtun (Aaron Nelson-Moody) from the Squamish Nation. Guess what adorns the figure's head? A proper copper topper.

108 Whistler Train Station

This ain't no Grand Central

As far as famous grandiose train stations around the world go, this one doesn't really rank. However, Whistler's current small, modern railway stop, which replaced the old one in 2007, is still significant.

The station was designed to fit in with the typical local architecture and it does that very well. It's actually an intriguing building made of wood and stone and conveniently located in Creekside next to the Nita Lake Lodge. A visit to the station is worth it just to look at the steel rails from overhead. That bird's-eye viewing point is on a uniquely raised covered bridge that crosses the tracks below. This platform also gives you a stunning elevated view of Whistler Mountain and the surrounding forest, and it creates a great first impression for the scarce disembarking passengers. The other unusual aspect of this station is that it is missing one very important element found in most train stations – trains. Today, the only passengers to see the station are riding the high-end luxury tourist train called the Rocky Mountaineer, which makes very limited periodic stops at the Whistler Station on its way to Jasper, Alberta.

With two million-plus visitors a year to Whistler, you'd think the station would be as crowded as Grand Central. But it's not. The line, which was completed by CPR in 1916, played a huge role in the development of local industry and the movement of freight, but a much smaller role in delivering skiers to Whistler. It's surprising because the scenery all the way from the train station in North Vancouver to Whistler is filled with amazing canyons, high wooden trestles, and breathtaking ocean views lining the route. In the 1970s and 1980s, small, crude, and slow BUDD Cars (a small train that is an engine and passenger compartment built into one car) serviced the route with a schedule that never really synced with skiers' needs, and as such became defunct.

Address 2029 London Lane, Whistler, BC V0N 1B2, +1 (877) 460-3200, www.viarail.ca/en/explore-our-destinations/stations/whistler-village | **Getting there** Heading south from Whistler Village on the Sea to Sky Highway, turn right onto Lake Placid Road to destination on the left. | **Hours** Unrestricted | **Tip** Having a fancy spa housed in a train station is oh-so-Whistler. Peer through the windows at The Spa at Nita Lake Lodge to see a striking wall with five large, vertical, live-edge pieces of beautiful wood above the pedicure chairs (2131 Lake Placid Road, www.nitalakelodge.com/spa).

109 Whistler Skate Park

It's sick!

Skateparks are much more than big cement spaces meant to keep noise, vandalism, loitering, and other negative traits associated with skateboarding off the streets. Good ones, like the Whistler Skate Park, are carefully crafted and engineered public facilities bringing people from all backgrounds together to pursue their passion for creativity, speed, exercise, self-expression, and social development. In other words, they're fun places to hang and chill.

Whistler's civic planners must have bought into this positive premise in 1991, when the town's original skatepark was constructed. To achieve their goal of building a really "sick" park, they called upon Monty Little and Terry Snider to design it. These two had fresh experience designing skateparks in North and West Vancouver. Little saw the Whistler Skatepark as a giant sculpture, taking inspiration from the mountains and streams of the area.

The park served the community well until the end of the 1990s, when it needed to be refurbished for safety reasons. The sport had evolved too, and new elements were added that were more in tune with the next generation of skateboarders. In order to facilitate the modern technical tricks and maneuvers of the period, rails and grindable edges were incorporated into the upgrade. The latest expansion and renovation of the skateboard park took place in 2016 and cost the community almost a million dollars.

Highlights of the new design include the serpentine run into the snake bowl, a unique feature in North America. A second area contains a variety of quarter pipes up to 3 metres (10 feet) high, a spine, a volcano, and a central pyramid. The park consists of over 4,600 square metres (50,000 square feet) of skateable surface, the second largest in Canada. When summer comes along and all the snow is long gone, locals trade their skis and snowboards for skateboards.

Address 4330 Blackcomb Way, Whistler, BC V0N 1B4, www.whistler.ca/culture-recreation/facilities/skate-park | **Getting there** From the Sea to Sky Highway, take the Village Gate exit and turn left on Blackcomb Way. Park at first right. | **Hours** Open 24 hours, outdoor lighting till 1am | **Tip** If you arrived in town without your skateboard, you can buy one at Whistler's first skate shop, the SK8 CAVE located in Function Junction (1208 Alpha Lake Road, No. 4, www.facebook.com/thesk8cave).

110 Whistling Marmots

How Whistler got its name

If bear spotting scares you (see ch. 11), here's another furry creature to consider observing at Whistler: the marmot. Marmots aren't as dangerous and have an even closer association with the mountain. To the untrained eye the marmot can be mistaken for a large beaver or even a small bear. Technically they're ground squirrels, but these critters are a lot bigger than your average squirrel, with large ones tipping the scales at a hefty 9 kilos (20 pounds). Marmots can be found all the way up to Alaska, although their habitats are mainly on the West Coast of British Columbia, Washington, and Oregon.

So how are these cute mountain creatures linked to Whistler's heritage? First you need a short primer on the history of the mountain's name. Up until the early 1960s, Whistler was known as London Mountain because of the heavy fog and mist of the coastal alpine region. London, England was of course famous for its thick fog. But low visibility, thick fog, and mist are not exactly descriptors you want if you're marketing an international winter destination. Ask most out-of-towners what Whistler is named after, and you'll get answers from the painting *Whistler's Mother* to the sound of a train whistle, or the mating call of a bluejay.

Wrong. It's marmots.

Marmots are known for the whistling sound they make when they are in danger or feel threatened, and Whistler has a huge population of them. They hibernate for 200 days a year, but in the summer marmots emit their curious high pitched whistling sound, to the joy of hikers nearby. A great place where you are almost guaranteed to see them is at the Rendezvous Lodge on top of Blackcomb. If you don't spot one, you will surely hear their distinctive whistle. Interpretive signs, special fencing to protect them, and friendly informative staff will assist you on your quest to hear Whistler's whistling marmots.

Address The Rendezvous Lodge, 4545 Blackcomb Way, Whistler, BC V0N 1B4, +1 (800) 766-0499, www.whistlerblackcomb.com | **Getting there** Take the Blackcomb Gondola to the top of Blackcomb Mountain. The Rendezvous is a short stroll away from where you exit. | **Hours** Daily 10am–4:30pm | **Tip** Blackcomb Mountain's 1.4-kilometres (1-mile) Alpine Walk Trail is said to be one of the best places to photograph marmots in the summer season. Wear sensible shoes and whistle while you walk (www.alltrails.com/trail/canada/british-columbia/alpine-walk-trail).

111 Yurt Camping

Yurt gonna love this kind of glamping

If you like to camp, but you don't like pitching tents and sleeping on the ground, you might want to try the yurts at Parkbridge Resort. The original yurts, tents used by ancient Mongolian nomads for thousands of years in Central Asia, are the inspiration for this unique camping experience. But don't worry – the 10 yurts here have had the full twentieth-century makeover. Rope has been replaced with aircraft-quality steel tension cables, and felt has been replaced with reflective insulation developed by top brains at NASA. Above the kiln-dried Douglas fir floors, rafters, and lattice walls, there's even a luxurious dome skylight that lets in lots of natural light. And there are windows, a proper door, a dining table, and even electric heat. Mongolian nomads may want to take note.

Thousands of travelers of all ages and from all over the world visit the Parkbridge Resort each year from Germany, France, China, Russia, Brazil, Africa, Australia, and so on. There's always someone interesting to meet. Some arrive here in RVs, others by car, and some even by bike.

In the summertime, the resorts' bike enthusiasts enjoy the roughly 1,000 kilometres (625 miles) of impressive mountain bike trails that cut through and around the Whistler Valley, including the 70-kilometres-long (44-mile), paved Valley Trail that connects the campsite to Whistler Village and is just a 10-minute bike ride away. Lost Lake is also a short ride or hike away – in addition to having a dog beach, it is a favorite place to enjoy one of Whistler's most-established traditions: getting naked. What better way to cool off on a sunny day than a quick skinny dip in an alpine lake?

Bike in the other direction and you can watch the float planes land at Green Lake or head over to the Parkhurst Ghost Town (see ch. 68). In the winter, you can rent snowshoes to explore the trails. The Scandinave Spa (see ch. 87) is a stone's throw away.

Address 8018 Mons Road, Whistler, BC V0N 1B8, +1 (604) 905-5533, www.parkbridge.com/en-ca/rv-cottages/riverside-resort/accommodations/yurts | **Getting there** From the Sea to Sky Highway, exit right at Spruce Grove Way, turn left onto Mons Road to the registration office. | **Hours** Office open daily 8am–10pm in summer, 9am–7pm in winter | **Tip** Riverside Junction Café, a short downhill walk from the Yurts, opens at 7am and serves a hearty breakfast and lunch (8018 Mons Road).

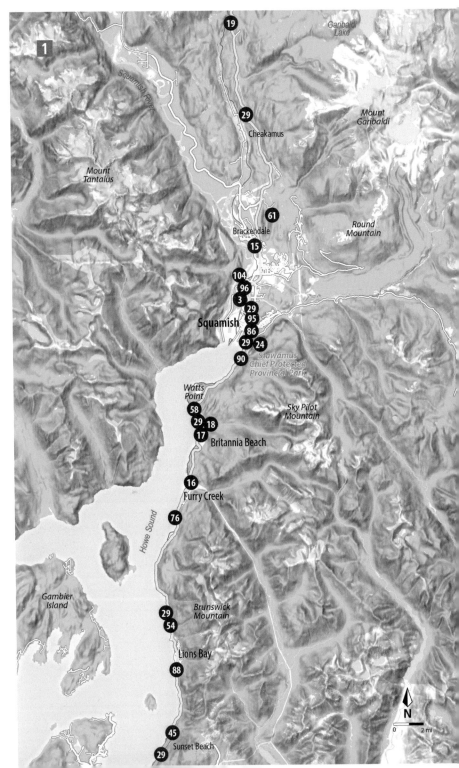

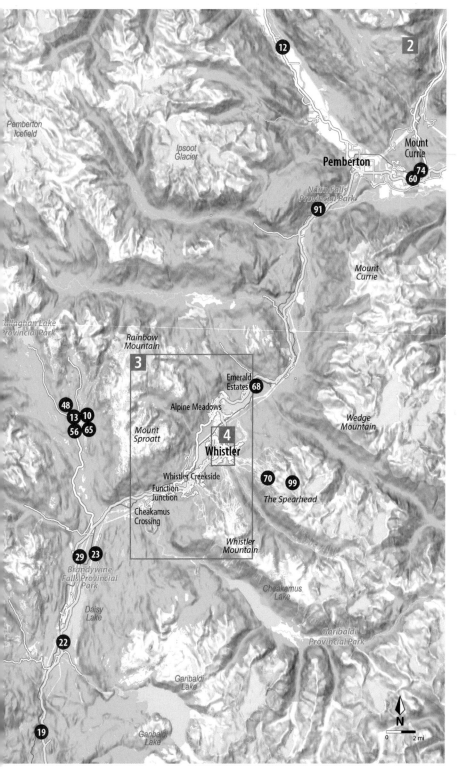

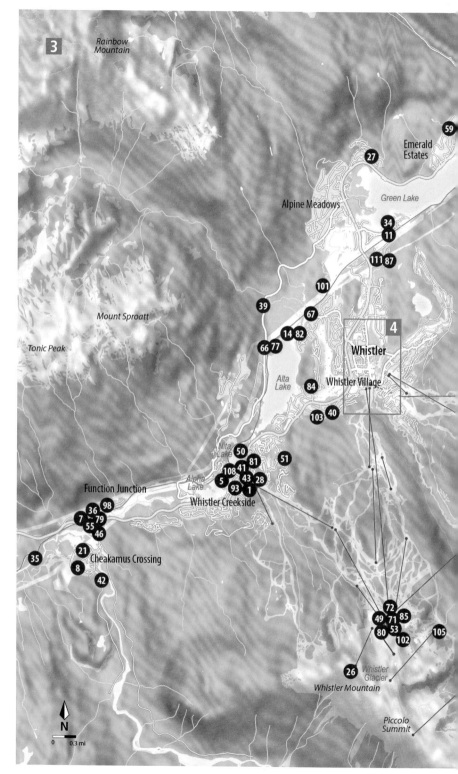

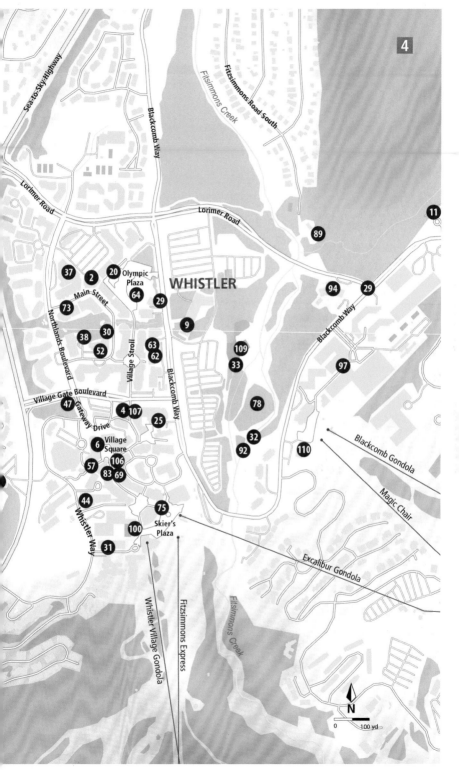

Dave Doroghy, Graeme Menzies
111 Places in Vancouver
That You Must Not Miss
ISBN 978-3-7408-0494-7

Jennifer Bain, Christina Ryan
111 Places in Calgary
That You Must Not Miss
ISBN 978-3-7408-0749-8

Anita Mai Genua, Clare Davenport,
Elizabeth Lenell Davies
111 Places in Toronto
That You Must Not Miss
ISBN 978-3-7408-0257-8

Jo-Anne Elikann
111 Places in New York
That You Must Not Miss
ISBN 978-3-95451-052-8

Kim Windyka, Heather Kapplow,
Alyssa Wood
111 Places in Boston
That You Must Not Miss
ISBN 978-3-7408-0894-5

Andréa Seiger, John Dean
111 Places in Washington
That You Must Not Miss
ISBN 978-3-7408-0258-5

Amy Bizzarri, Susie Inverso
111 Places in Chicago
That You Must Not Miss
ISBN 978-3-7408-0156-4

Katrina Nattress, Jason Quigley
111 Places in Portland
That You Must Not Miss
ISBN 978-3-7408-0750-4

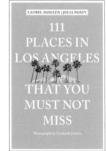

Laurel Moglen, Julia Posey,
Lyudmila Zotova
111 Places in Los Angeles
That You Must Not Miss
ISBN 978-3-95451-884-5

Floriana Petersen,
Steve Werney
**111 Places in San Francisco
That You Must Not Miss**
ISBN 978-3-95451-609-4

Floriana Petersen,
Steve Werney
**111 Places in Silicon Valley
That You Must Not Miss**
ISBN 978-3-7408-0493-0

Christoph Hein, Sabine Hein
**111 Places in Singapore
That You Shouldn't Miss**
ISBN 978-3-7408-0382-7

John Sykes, Birgit Weber
**111 Places in London
That You Shouldn't Miss**
ISBN 978-3-95451-346-8

Kai Oidtmann
**111 Places in Iceland
That You Shouldn't Miss**
ISBN 978-3-7408-0030-7

Andrea Livnat,
Angelika Baumgartner
**111 Places in Tel Aviv
That You Shouldn't Miss**
ISBN 978-3-7408-0263-9

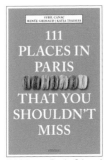

Sybil Canac, Renée Grimaud,
Katia Thomas
**111 Places in Paris
That You Shouldn't Miss**
ISBN 978-3-7408-0159-5

Alexia Amvrazi,
Diana Farr Louis, Diane Shugart,
Yannis Varouhakis
**111 Places in Athens
That You Shouldn't Miss**
ISBN 978-3-7408-0377-3

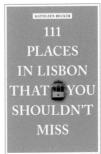

Kathleen Becker
**111 Places in Lisbon
That You Shouldn't Miss**
ISBN 978-3-7408-0383-4

Thanks to all the people who helped us nail down the million and one details that writing a book like this requires. Special thanks again to our editor Karen Seiger for granting us a couple of much-needed pandemic deadline extensions, and to Laura Olk, and all the folks at Emons, for their hard work and dedication to the *111 Places* series.

Additional thanks are owed to friends old and new for their ideas, suggestions, hospitality, generosity, and patience: Peter Zell, Brian Antonson, Miriam Soet, Doug Forseth, Paul Shore, Maureen Douglas, Mark McCurdy, Sharon Denny, Gary Cadman, Baird Menzies, Angedd Kalsi, Steve Podborski, Peter Varsek, Mariko Nakagawa, Paula Jeffers, Jeff Oldenborger, Hillary Davidson, Dan Ellis, Father Andrew L'Heureux, Tyler Brown, Dave Williams, Harvey Lim, Silke Jeltsch, Capt. Cheryl Major, Yvonne Chiang, Kristen Jones, Chris Webster, Kirsten Jones, Patrick Sills, Marc Des Rosiers, Kim Ebers, Kanna Martin, Lynne Cook, Emma Sturdy, Tyler Schramm, Russell Kling, Aaron Lawton, Clark Gatehouse, Hannah Stock, Mandy Rousseau, Alison Pascal, Erin Copeland, Sean Tremblay, Luke Snyder, Shane Holland, Gordon Bell, Xwalacktun (Rick Harry), Jeff Venoit, Brad Nichols and Allyn Pringle and the staff at the Whistler Museum, Jennifer Smith and Vail Resorts, Claire Van Leeuwen and the Resort Municipality of Whistler, Maelle Cote and Chad "Junior" Millett at Black's Pub, and Pangea Pod Hotel model Georgina Stokes. And special thanks to Jeannie Page for her help and support.

Dave Doroghy has visited over 50 different countries with pen in hand and camera strapped around his neck and like many Vancouverites, he has skied at Whistler since we was a teenager. His careers have spanned radio broadcasting, advertising and finally 20 years in sports marketing where he was the Vice President of the former NBA Vancouver Grizzlies and was the Director of Sponsorship Sales for the Vancouver 2010 Olympic Winter Games. Dave shares his time between Whistler and Vancouver. He is co-author of *111 Places in Vancouver That You Must Not Miss*, and author of *Show Me The Honey: Adventures of an Accidental Apiarist*. He also co-hosts a weekly podcast with Graeme Menzies called "Vancouver and Whistler Places."

Graeme Menzies has lived in seven cities across Canada, in the United States, England, and Brazil, but still thinks the Sea to Sky area of British Columbia is unparalleled in its beauty and character. An international marketing and communications professional with past experience in the arts, public policy, technology, the 2010 Winter Olympics, and higher education, Graeme's curiosity fuels his passion for discovering new places and for shedding new light on old ones. He is co-author of *111 Places in Vancouver That You Must Not Miss*. He also co-hosts a weekly podcast with Dave Doroghy called "Vancouver and Whistler Places."